The Science of Reading People:
How to Understand What People Are Really Saying and Why

By Patrick King
Social Interaction and Conversation Coach at
www.PatrickKingConsulting.com

Table of Contents

SECTION 1   7

CHAPTER 1: WHAT STOPS US FROM ACCURATELY PERCEIVING OTHERS?   7

CHAPTER 2: THE ART OF PERSPECTIVE TAKING   27

CHAPTER 3: THE FOUR PERSONALITY TYPES AND "PERCEPTUAL POSITIONS"   35

SECTION 2   57

CHAPTER 4: THE FOUR FUNCTIONS OF BEHAVIOR   57

CHAPTER 5: LEARNING TO READ EMOTIONS   75

CHAPTER 6: BASELINING   95

CHAPTER 7: WATCH WARDROBE, WALK, AND FOOD   113

SECTION 3 — 135

CHAPTER 8: NLP AND PEOPLE'S META-PROGRAMMING — 135

CHAPTER 9: KEEP YOUR EARS PRICKED FOR WORD CLUES — 161

CHAPTER 10: THE ART OF ASKING THE RIGHT QUESTIONS — 187

Section 1

Chapter 1: What Stops Us from Accurately Perceiving Others?

The first step to really reading a person? Pay attention!

You'd be surprised how much you can see if you only look. But by the same token, many of us don't see what is right in front of us because there is something in the way of our perception. "Perceptual barriers" interfere with our accurate perception of others. This seems obvious, but it's a point worth laboring—if you only perceive what you want to, it's as good as not perceiving at all. That means that **if you can remove bias, expectation, assumption, ego, prejudice, interpretation, judgment—in short, as much of your subjectivity as possible—**

then the better you will be at reading people.

Here are some of the things you may not realize are undermining your ability to really understand other people.

Perceptual Selectivity

Simply, this is the tendency to choose certain objects from the environment while ignoring others. An individual's pre-existing beliefs, values, and needs determine which objects are focused on. Being selective means that your perception is more influenced by your own attitudes, interests, and background than by the stimulus itself. To really see what is in front of them, a person must screen out most stimuli and focus on only a few—but *how* they do this makes a world of difference.

Importantly, being selective is not a huge problem—we all do it. Rather, we need to be aware of when it's happening so we don't confuse our own conclusions with reality. For example, let's say we are in an ambiguous situation. Someone is suddenly upset. We think, "Must be that time of the month," and congratulate ourselves for being great at reading between the lines.

Can you see the problem? Your selective focus on one aspect of the situation (the person being female), combined with your own beliefs and assumptions, has led you to make a guess about someone that is probably distorted. In this case, you are more accurately perceiving your own intellectual shortcuts rather than something objectively in your environment.

Attribution

Attribution is what we do when we try to explain why people behave as they do. For example, we see a child having a tantrum and think, "He's deliberately trying to push my buttons." We've made a guess as to the cause and motivation of the behavior. It's normal to draw conclusions about the factors that influence people, or try to make meaning of their behavior. We all like to feel that the world makes a certain sense and that we can reliably predict the behavior of others. But again, in this way, our own bias may creep in and obscure what is actually happening. We are too busy seeing what we know is there that we cannot see what *is* there!

Imagine this example. You are talking to a person from Japan. They have made a mistake. You've brought it to their attention, and now they are grinning at you and nodding furiously. If you did this yourself, it would mean one thing only: You didn't take the situation seriously and were even laughing rudely at the other person. So you ask yourself the question, "Why are they behaving this way?" But you answer the question as though you were answering for *yourself*: "Because they don't take this seriously." In fact, it's just a cultural difference. The Japanese often smile in awkward situations in order to defuse tension—it is the opposite of rudeness!

Stereotyping

That is, judging someone based on what you think about the group to which they belong. It is a basic human trait to see a person as part of a single group or class, and then to give that person positive or negative traits based on what most people think about that group as a whole. It's one of the ways we simplify our world and make it easier to understand. It's also a surefire way to distort our perception of how people actually are—

and they're usually a lot more complex than stereotypes would suggest.

Have you ever been really surprised to learn that a person you thought you knew was actually quite different from what you first thought? It's a great opportunity to ask why your expectations were so subverted. **Stereotypes don't have to be full-blown prejudices to distort perception**. In fact, our perception can be most disturbed by those assumptions we have that are usually true. For example, a drug-trafficking operation could work precisely because it employs the help of unassuming elderly women to transport packages. The stereotype that little old ladies don't smuggle heroin is pretty accurate—but believing it will allow you to miss the truth.

The Halo Effect

Speaking of little old ladies, **the "halo effect" is the tendency to judge people based on a single trait, whether that trait is good or bad**. The halo effect is very similar to stereotyping. However, in stereotyping, a person is judged by the group they belong to, while with the halo effect, they are judged by a single trait they possess.

We sometimes judge a person based on the first thing we see or hear about them. For instance, if someone is kind, they may also be seen as trustworthy, competent, hardworking, and so on. If someone is beautiful, we might wrongly assume that they are also healthy or intelligent, or if rich we might imagine they are materialistic or have good taste. We might see a tech billionaire with an interest in economics, politics, or social issues, and wrongly assume that if they possess a certain business acumen, they must somehow also be adept in other areas.

In real life and with real people, these traits sometimes go together, and sometimes they don't. A celebrity may have something relevant to share about animal rights or the best diet for children, but they may also be just as ignorant as the next person. By the same token, there is nothing to say that a doctor who goes to prison for assault suddenly knows any less about medicine than he did before (let's call it a "devil horns" effect!) or that people who are color blind can't be good artists. In either case, if we take one observation and over-extrapolate it, we stop perceiving what is actually happening in front of us.

Projection

Sometimes, we perceive not what somebody is, but what *we* are—we project onto them the same way a film projector puts its image onto a screen. This idea originally comes from the theories of Carl Jung, who explained how people might disidentify with some unwanted traits, and then seem to discover them in other people.

But projection doesn't have to be a serious psychological phenomenon involving shadows and unconscious material. Sometimes it simply occurs because **people lazily assume that others are more like themselves than they really are**.

Have you ever been surprised to find that someone you knew actually had very different religious or political opinions than you originally believed? You might have enjoyed their company and simply assumed that what they thought was the same as what you thought. So there is some stimulus in the environment and you wrongly assume what their response will be. Or you observe some behavior in them and automatically conclude a cause for this behavior that is more accurately a cause for *your* behavior, not theirs.

Perceptual Set

A perceptual set is a group of beliefs about how others see and understand certain situations. For example, a manager may come to believe and act as if workers are lazy and just want to get as much as they can from the organization without giving their best. This is a mix of different assumptions, preconceptions, and ideas—it's a set. Another example is when a family has a perceptual set for one child that includes a whole narrative about them being special, unique, and precious, while the perceptual set for the other child revolves around their being difficult and troubled.

You can tell a perceptual set is in play because it tends to distort neutral stimuli so that it fits the set, rather than realizing that the set is inaccurate. For example, the "black sheep" described in the family above may often behave in intelligent, kind, and unexpected ways, but this behavior will be interpreted so that it *always supports the pre-*

existing perceptual set. The parents might perceive this behavior, but say, "Every once in a while, he does stunts like this just to show off. He's always been egotistical like that. He's just looking for attention, as usual."

Implicit Personality Theory

When judging and making assumptions about other people, a person's thoughts are affected by **how he thinks certain human traits are linked to each other**. This is something you might never have given a second thought—but can you be sure that the "rules" you assume control the way personality traits cluster are actually accurate?

Later, we'll see that personality theories have been a perennial fascination for social theorists, psychologists, and lay people-readers since time began. But an *implicit* personality theory is the (often unexamined, unconscious, and inaccurate) model of what personalities are and how they are formed.

For example, hard work is often linked to being honest. People think that anyone who works hard must be honest. Have you ever made this implicit association? If someone told you that someone at work had been stealing petty cash, wouldn't you tend to suspect the lazier members of the team over the workaholics and "Type A" people? It's because you're working with a model that assumes the traits go together.

But if you examine this association, you'll see that there's no reason at all that one implies the other. If you don't believe it's possible for someone to share *both* traits, or neither, then you stop being able to accurately perceive that person when they cross your path.

Expectancy

Expectation is the tendency to see people, things, and events based on how we thought they would be in the first place. Imagine you're about to be introduced to someone you are told is a priest. You know very little about priests and have no experience with them, but you immediately start assuming things: They're stern, maybe a bit of a killjoy, upright, softly spoken, middle-aged, kind of boring, morally superior, compassionate, or perhaps they are hiding a terrible secret.

When you actually meet the priest, your expectations mean you are unconsciously looking for confirmation of all this. You discount all the things that don't line up with the picture you already have in your head. The things that do line up, you focus on and even encourage. This situation is why this is sometimes also called a "self-fulfilling prophecy."

Let's say you believe that priests are all compassionate and non-judgmental. When you meet, you start confessing all your personal troubles. The priest sees that someone needs his attention, and politely gives it. You think, "See? Priests are compassionate." However, if you hadn't led the priest down that path by confessing so much, you might have discovered that he would have preferred to talk about Formula One racing.

Perceptual Defense

One final thing to consider is that **we may not be able to accurately perceive people simply because what they are or what they are saying are actually too threatening to acknowledge fully.** Here, "threatening" can encompass a broad range of ideas. It can mean subtle but culturally unacceptable ideas that your mind unconsciously chooses not to see. Have you ever noticed that some people can be very obviously gay, and yet many people around them seem oblivious to the fact? Their eyes work; it's just that they don't really want to see!

It can go the other way, too. If someone is very anxious and suspicious, anything their partner does may be perceived as strange and troubling. In the first example, the defense is not to perceive fully; in the second example, the defense is to see things that aren't actually there. In both cases, the perception is not accurate. A little perceptual defense is only human, and sometimes it's necessary. For example, we don't tell little kids that it's impossible for them to become astronauts—a little modification of a harsh truth is sometimes necessary!

Improving Your Perceptual Accuracy

As you can see, one thing continually gets in the way of accurate perception: ourselves! **All the above share something in common: We prioritize our idea about reality over reality itself.** Anytime we do this, we undermine our powers of perception. So how do we get better?

1. Know thyself

Knowing who you are is a powerful way to avoid perceptual distortions. It lets you know what is *your* stuff, and what is *their* stuff. What values, beliefs, and blind spots do you bring to the table? To be a good people-reader, you don't have to completely remove these blind spots—you just need to be honest about the fact that they are there.

Overwhelmingly, people usually see others wrong because they don't see themselves right. The better a person knows himself, the better he can understand other people. Importantly, don't just flesh out your idea of who you *want* to be, or focus only on the good. Instead, be clear about all that other stuff, too—prejudices, fears, bad habits, and so on.

A good question to ask yourself is, what are your most recurrent personal biases and prejudices? If you say "none," then there is work to do! We all have them. Know what yours are. For example, if you are aware that you tend to assume that everyone is less intelligent than you are, be honest about how this skews your perception. What can you routinely do to offset this tendency?

2. Cultivate empathy

We tend to think of empathy and kindness as more or less the same thing. But empathy has a perceptual and cognitive component. It means not merely caring about how others feel, but actually understanding it and being able to perceive it. After all, how can you care and be kind if you don't even know what is happening, or why?

Empathy is a natural trait, but it's also a skill one can develop over time with the help of a good feedback system and genuine interactions with others. Don't simply assume you are already empathetic enough. Constantly check that your perceptions about others are actually true—or else you risk becoming one of those people who crows about being an "empath" but who really, really isn't!

Something to try: Get into the habit of *asking, not assuming*. For example, if you're worried one day that you've offended someone, don't just take it as a given that you have. Don't just assume that your guess about their inner perception is 100 percent accurate. Confirm your reading of the situation by asking them. Empathy is not all about mind-reading—sometimes good old-fashioned communication leads to far more understanding!

3. Be positive

Perceptions are strongly and long-lastingly affected by how people feel. When we have a bad opinion of someone or something, our view of that person or thing will be skewed. Furthermore, if we have a bad opinion of *ourselves* or of life in general, that cannot help but color the way we see the person in front of us.

"Positive" here doesn't mean rose-colored glasses, but rather a kind of gentle, curious, open-minded optimism that is secure enough to allow us to abandon our own preferences so we can more clearly see the way things really are. It's the wholesome attitude of, "Hm, here is a new person I know nothing about. I wonder what I'm going to learn about them?"

A good habit to practice: When dealing with someone you find difficult, routinely ask yourself "What is working right now?" This will train you to see possibility, options, solutions, and avenues you hadn't considered. Be willing to learn. If someone says something that seems totally wrong, ask what is right about it. Assume there *is* something. Ask how their perspective is enriching you. Ask what you can learn from any difference between you. Ask what that potential friction could be showing you about your own limitations.

4. Postpone Impression Formation

People have a natural tendency to quickly form strong opinions about things or people. Just from one or two meetings, we can figure out what someone is like. Though this is an understandable part of human nature, we often sacrifice accuracy for speed and ease. But just remind yourself of how annoying it is to be pigeon-holed by others based on just one or two of your traits. **Deliberately make the effort to just *wait*—you don't have to**

form an opinion about everything! Let people show you who they are. It takes time.

Here's a great habit to cultivate: Change statements to questions. This will keep you curious and open-minded and will improve your perception. The moment you form a conclusion about someone, your perception is out of the game and you go into *assumption* instead! For example, notice yourself wanting to say "She's a snob," and turn it into a question. "Is she a snob?" This simple shift allows you to notice the possibility that you could interpret her behavior in some other way. It helps you notice what is happening, rather than you focusing on your premature *theory* about what is happening.

5. Practice open communication

Many misunderstandings are caused by poor or one-way communication. Or, let's be honest, a complete lack of communication. A whole world of perceptual distortions can appear in a conversation if we are not conscious of how we send and receive information.

One good idea: don't ask leading questions. Instead, ask with a genuinely open and curious mind and truly listen to what you're told. Imagine that you are not asking questions to confirm or disprove a running hypothesis, but are genuinely wanting to learn something . . . and perhaps even be surprised.

To run with the previous example, you might ask the woman who always insists on wearing cashmere, wool, and silk to tell you more about why she does this. You learn that she's not a snob at all, but has a skin allergy that makes wearing synthetic fabrics impossible.

6. Verify your perceptions by comparing them with others

One way to reduce perceptual errors is to compare how you see something to how someone else sees it. You may have already done this in the past and were shocked at the discrepancy! By talking about how we see things, we learn about different points of view and may be able to understand the situation much better.

That said, comparing our perceptions with others doesn't mean they're right and we're wrong; rather, it's an exercise in perspective taking. In the same way that certain colors tend to change depending on what colors they appear next to, comparison can bring to light certain assumptions we didn't know we were making.

Chapter 2: The Art of Perspective Taking

Perspective taking is the ability to imagine another person's psychological viewpoint. When we are very young children, we actually don't know how to do this—it is a human skill that needs to be learned like any other. It requires stepping outside one's self-centeredness to genuinely see things from another's perspective. Not see that person's situation through your own eyes, but see their situation as *they* would see it, through their eyes.

Empathy is about imagining what a person perceives, thinks, and feels as themselves. Perspective taking naturally leads to imagining what another person would *do*. We can predict their behavior because we more thoroughly understand their motivations. **"Theory of mind" is the ability**

to imagine someone else's mental state, even if it differs from our own.

The fashion designer Oscar de la Renta is said to have once advised women: "Walk like there are three men walking behind you." From his point of view, he imagined what it was like to be a woman and concluded that if there were three men walking behind you, you would probably walk in a sexier way. But women were quick to point out that when they heard this advice, they were confused. If three men were walking behind them, they said, they might not be feeling sexy but cautious and alert. They'd walk faster or even cross to the other side of the road.

De la Renta illustrates here a common blind spot—he was not imagining what it would be like to be a woman, but rather imagining what it would be like for him, as a man, to be a woman . . . big difference! Perhaps he had seen women in the street, thought they were sexy, then concluded that this experience of them as sexy was identical to what they were experiencing. His perception on the entire thing was distorted. He was unable to genuinely abandon his perspective and take up another.

Everybody *thinks* they have empathy, the ability to perspective-switch and find true understanding, but in truth they seldom do. Our insistence that we can properly see others actually prevents us from doing so! But here are some ways to sincerely practice walking in another person's shoes—and not in the way that Oscar de la Renta does!

Tip 1: Watch a movie or TV show

Getting into movies or TV shows is a great way to learn how to see things from other people's points of view. Many believe reading fiction helps you really get into other people's feelings and see events from their points of view, but the same thing can be done with film—literally you are forced to take a certain angle on a situation.

When you want to see something from someone else's point of view, pick a movie or TV show and choose a character's point of view. You can even begin with a character who reminds you of yourself. As you get better at putting yourself in other people's shoes, try to ask yourself certain questions as you watch:

- What are they thinking, and why?

- Why are they behaving as they are?
- What are they trying to achieve?
- What emotions are they experiencing, and why?
- How are they explaining the situation to themselves?
- What aspects of the situation are most salient for them?

One of the problems with studying people this way is that it can be tricky to know if you've missed the mark or not. But a few questions can help you assess your reading:

- Were you able to understand the events on screen in a deeper way? In other words, could you more easily predict the ending or understand the character's choices? Did you feel like the story and the character "made sense"?
- Could you clearly see and articulate the reasons the character did what he or she did?
- Could you feel the emotions the character portrayed and point to where they came from?

Another problem is that not all film and TV is created equal. Practice this often enough and you may find your tastes changing because you more frequently spot a poorly developed character!

Tip 2: Use your (social) imagination

Imagining hypothetical situations, like one does in role-play, is another good way to think about things from different points of view. The key is to really inject yourself into different roles and fully inhabit them. Little children do this when they play with dolls, alternatively speaking for each one. Practice a similar exercise and you can develop your social imagination.

Find a picture of people engaging in a dynamic scene—look at magazines, photos, movie stills, etc. Look closely at the image and try to imagine a dramatic story to accompany it. What came before, and what will come after? What's going on and how do each of the people feel about it?

For example, if one person in the story is holding a gun, ask yourself how they feel and try to really imagine being them in that moment. Are they scared, angry? How do the other people seem to this person? What are they focusing most on in the scene? What are they trying to achieve, and how?

Now switch and inhabit the point of view of another person in the image. How does their perspective compare? What do they think of the person with the gun? As you can see, there are many layers to this—not just comprehending other people's emotions, but their assessment of the emotions of people around them, and so on. We'll explore this more deeply in the next chapter.

Tip 3: Switch perspectives in your own life

Take a moment to recall a recent misunderstanding, argument, or conflict. In the same way as you did above, try to hold a snapshot of this in your mind's eye, then deliberately switch between points of view, almost like you were changing radio stations. What does the problem look like from the other person's perspective? How do you appear to them? If you're finding this exercise difficult, don't worry—it *is* difficult! Try answering these questions to deepen your insight:

- What has objectively happened?

- What has each person focused on in this situation?
- What is everyone's motivation?
- How do you think everyone feels?
- How is each person making sense of what is going on? How do they explain it?
- What do they think about *your* role—is it accurate?
- How does each person frame the issue?

Though perspective taking is great for improving communication and helping smooth over conflict, it can be applied to improving our people-reading skills, too. The idea is that if we can fully understand *how a person sees things*, we understand more about them on a fundamental level. The reverse is true, also—if we know who they are, we can more accurately understand how things will appear to them.

Chapter 3: The Four Personality Types and "Perceptual Positions"

When trying to read and analyze people, it's human nature to simplify things and set out to understand what "kind" of person we are looking at. What category do they belong to? Centuries ago, in medieval times, people spoke about how the "humors" of the body determined personality (some people could be "choleric" or "sanguine," etc., according to the functions of their dominant organs), and in ancient Ayurveda, a person's physiological constitution also told you a lot about their attitude, intelligence, and emotions.

To this day, people continue to be captivated by the idea of what makes each of us unique—by putting us in groups with others who are similar! We also seem to be interested in where our psychological traits come from and how they're grouped, not just so we understand others better, but also so we understand ourselves.

More recently, the Myers-Briggs Type Indicator (MBTI) and the Enneagram have become the personality assessment frameworks that capture the modern desire to put people in categories. Typically, some fundamental human characteristics are identified and then combined in a matrix that yields a limited set of possible types.

One notable personality theory to understand is what's called the Big Five, or the OCEAN model. This is a long-standing framework in personality assessment that is used by psychologists the world over. A person can score high or low on each of these main factors:

Openness – Your natural curiosity and readiness to learn and experience new things.
Conscientiousness – How thoughtful, considerate, or dependable you are.
Extraversion – How outgoing, sociable, and assertive you are in social situations.
Agreeableness – Your willingness to be sympathetic, accommodating, and

cooperative with other people, and your broad concern/sympathy for them.
Neuroticism – Your emotional style and the likeliness of emotional instability, mood swings, depression, loneliness, anger, or sadness.

Whichever model you use, though, the idea is that if you know a person's type, you immediately have deeper insight into what makes them tick.

But it's worth remembering that personality theories and frameworks of this kind are just that—models. That means that they are necessarily limited. We continue to propose new frameworks, however. In 2018, Northwestern University's Luis Amaral and colleagues conducted a worldwide survey. Participant data on personalities and traits were collected from all around the world using a questionnaire, and the results were synthesized in the research.

The researchers then looked at the data of more than 1.5 million people who'd taken part in personality tests, and started plotting where they scored on each of the Big Five factors. Examining the patterns in their data, they managed to identify four main personality types, i.e., the most recurrent patterns of scoring on the Big Five factors—**"average," "reserved," "self-centered," and "role model."** Their new personality types look like this:

Average
- The most common personality type
- High scores in both neuroticism and extraversion—these people tend to be more sociable and assertive, but also fairly pessimistic and oversensitive
- Low scores in openness—they're likely to be more routine-based, suspicious, conventional, and less open to abstraction
- These people tend to seek attention, but are not overly intellectually curious
- More likely to be women

Reserved
- Higher scores of agreeableness and conscientiousness—these are people who tend to be more trusting, sensitive, well-liked, and reliable
- Lower scores for both openness and neuroticism—this means they are not as open-minded and curious, but once

on a path, they stay the course with confidence and reliability
- Low neuroticism also means they're more emotionally stable and get on well with others
- Somewhat extroverted, but not overly so

Role Models
- High scores in extraversion, openness, agreeableness, and conscientiousness—these are the people who tend to exhibit qualities that evoke respect and admired leadership, and which allow them to cultivate good relationships with others
- Low scores in neuroticism—they are fairly confident and brave, taking calculated risks
- High conscientiousness and openness means they are dependable and open to new ideas
- They tend to be strong leaders
- More likely to be women

Self-Centered
- High scores in extraversion—such personalities are often very socially confident, energetic, and outgoing

- Low scores in openness, agreeableness, and conscientiousness—so they may be impulsive, headstrong, bad-tempered, rude/insensitive, and fixed to their routines
- Typically a self-serving attitude at the expense of others

The findings for the above four groups were published in the journal *Nature Human Behavior*. The researchers' claim was that the four types clustered predictably in the way they ranked the five different OCEAN traits. That means that the data consistently suggested that there were four recurrent ways in which people scored on the different aspects—rather than it being completely random.

So, what does that mean for the person who wants to master their people-reading skills? Well, simple: it means that your job suddenly got a whole lot easier!

Consider an example. You meet someone for the first time, and you notice a few things about them:

- It's a woman

- She mentions interacting with her family and friends a lot (i.e., seems close to them and therefore pretty sociable and extroverted) but always in the context of some sort of drama or dilemma (i.e., pretty high on neuroticism, too)
- When you mention something she says she's never heard about before, you notice that she shows no subsequent interest in it, preferring to steer the conversation back to familiar things instead of asking questions (i.e., low openness)
- You notice her make a little joke about pretending to be ill to get out of work (i.e., potentially low or average on conscientiousness)

Now, if you looked at all the above clues and came to the conclusion that you were dealing with an "average" personality type, would it be guaranteed that you were correct? Of course not. But as the evidence mounts, your hypothesis certainly becomes stronger. You may be dealing with the sort of person who has a rare blend of scores on each of the five traits. But it's not *likely*.

The researchers who proposed these four personality types were making probability claims—they used computational methods to analyze the data of 1.5 million people, and they found stable trends. That means that their findings can help you identify the most *likely* outcome—but never with 100 percent accuracy. But these four personality types are a great starting point.

If you identify one, you can always use that as your "working model" and continue to observe in order to learn more about the person in front of you. If this woman suddenly tells you that she actually used to be a UN goodwill ambassador and that she founded her own charity, you might adjust your assessment and look for further clues that she is actually closer to the "role model" type.

As you read and observe people, you are not just coming to conclusions and piecing clues together, you are also eliminating possibilities. For example, the researchers claim that teenage boys tend to be more highly represented in the "self-centered" category, and less so in the "role model" category. If you one day meet a teenage boy who is extremely low in agreeableness, then you can find out more about who he is by seeing who he *isn't*: Being low in agreeableness rules out the "role model" and "reserved" categories, leaving only "average" or "self-centered." Let's say that, due to him being a teenage boy, you *temporarily* assume he is in the "self-centered" category. But this is only temporary—when you get more data, you can rule out either one and be left with the most likely category.

You could still be completely wrong. But you are probably closer to the truth!

The researchers for this study also point out that even though they've identified some stable patterns in personality clusters, this doesn't mean that personality itself is static—i.e., that it never changes over the course of human development. The teenager above may find that puberty makes him temporarily less agreeable and conscientious, and his youth may make him more extroverted and energetic. But, in twenty years' time, he may morph into an enviable "role model" type. Likewise, he may be far more neurotic at school, but less so at home, where he is more comfortable. His personality didn't change, exactly; it just shifted a little given the change in environment. Finally, a person may enhance or downplay certain aspects of their character simply because they are in our company. We can all imagine that a teenage boy would find himself being a little more agreeable and conscientious if he was in the company of a girl he had a crush on and wanted to impress!

We don't need to worry too much about this, however. All we can ever do is perceive the information in front of us in whatever moment we find ourselves in. The next time you are trying to read and understand a person from scratch, ask yourself a few of the following questions to narrow things down a bit:

- Are they generally high in everything except openness? They're probably **average**.
- If they're high in everything, low in openness but don't seem to be neurotic—they're probably **reserved**.
- Do they seem not very open-minded but neither extroverted nor introverted? Again **reserved**—don't let the ordinary meaning of "reserved" fool you!

- Do they appear high in everything but unusually calm, content, and stable emotionally? A clear sign they are **role models**.
- Do they seem low in everything except extraversion? Probably **self-centered**.
- Do they seem kind of average in everything? They might be **reserved** (*not* average, which scores quite high on most traits).
- Do they seem kind of volatile and emotional (awkward, cynical, fearful, unconfident, insecure, and defensive)? They're probably **average** (interesting, isn't it, that high scores on neuroticism are actually most common?).
- Not extroverted? They're likely **reserved**—the only ones who consistently score low on extraversion.
- Are they open-minded and willing to experience new things? They're **role models**—again, the only category that consistently scores high on this trait. If you see it, it's a sure sign you're talking to a role model.

One final word on these traits: despite the impression the categories may give, there are no strict "good" traits or "bad" ones. For example, if you are extremely agreeable, you might find yourself being a bit of a doormat or a people-pleaser, or having poor boundaries. Being too open to experience may make you a little naïve and open for deception and manipulation. Being too conscientious can lead to stress, guilt, or weird codependent dynamics with others (i.e., those who are extremely low on conscientiousness!). By the same token, a little "neuroticism" is great if it allows us to properly assess risk, speak our truth, and assert our healthy boundaries.

But there's another reason it's important to remember not to make value judgments when we observe and read others: We risk distorting our perception. For example, if we personally think that extroverts are kind of annoying and superficial, we might notice this in someone and develop a "perceptual set," stereotype, or expectation about them that colors everything else we perceive. If we have an unconscious preference for introversion or think that this is the "right" way to be, then we are jeopardizing our people-reading accuracy.

Perceptual Positions

Let's see if we can combine what we know about personality types with what we know about perspective taking.

The perceptual positions framework is a basic method for understanding another person's viewpoint. Perceptual positions are a form of modeling that allows us to step into somebody else's shoes, see what they see, hear what they hear, and feel what they feel.

The technique comes from NLP—neurolinguistic programing—and has plenty of uses, including defusing conflict, fostering empathy, learning more about yourself, communicating well, and, of course, reading and analyzing people more effectively. If we combine it with a good personality theory, we can rapidly learn a lot about a person.

There are three perceptual positions: the first, the second, and the third (also called the observer or meta-position). Your task is to analyze or read a situation *from these different positions*. Doing so gives you so much more information (and empathy) and brings extra dimension to the entire encounter. Importantly, you are not just thinking about the things when in any position—you are engaging *all* your senses, so that you are considering what you smell, see, touch, etc. Let's look more closely.

First Position

This is like the "I" frame. It's the world as you see it through your own perceptual filters—a natural place to start. To flesh out this position, though, consider your perceptions on all five senses and become fully associated and embodied here. You'd be surprised at just how much you can learn about others in a situation when you more clearly understand where *you* are in the interaction.

Second Position

Also thought of as "the other" position. It's the ability to see the same situation that is seen by the person in the first position, but through their personal filters. This is a natural place to be for therapists and coaches, but also salespeople and those trying to persuade or motivate. Here, we are not associated, but dissociated and imagining someone else's perceptions.

Third Position

This is where we see the world through the "observer" filter, like a fly on the wall observing the interaction from outside the interaction. We are objective here and pass no judgment. This position is not actually involved in the unfolding story—i.e., the bigger but more neutral perspective. We are not associated or dissociated, but entirely independent.

Now, all this may seem pretty abstract until it's taken and put into context. It's nothing more complicated than a way to switch lenses as you view reality. Let's look at an example to show how the model can be applied.

Step 1

Think about a situation, problem, or conversation. Look at this situation from your own point of view. Flesh out your perspective and associate with it fully, on all five senses. It can be useful to describe the entire experience in one word.

For example, you are having an issue with a brother—you have invited him to stay, he's invited a friend you neither know well nor particularly like, and now things are awkward. You begin by fully inhabiting your own perspective: You see the intrusion of this unexpected person, feel an obligation to play host, but definitely realize that you'd prefer that the friend weren't there. One word: put upon (Okay, that's two words, but you get the picture).

Step 2

Look at the very same situation but from someone else's viewpoint. Do this *as them*—not as yourself imagining them. Big difference! If you were talking to a child, for example, and you were taking the second position and imagining their perception, literally picture what it's like to be small and look up at a taller adult—you. Find a single word to describe the experience from this perspective too.

In our example, you might do this both for your brother's point of view and for their friend. You do this as fully and genuinely as you can. In your brother's shoes, you feel fine—you like this person, so why wouldn't other people?

You are happy to see your brother, and you're relieved you get to have a friend nearby to keep you company (yup, you're feeling a little anxious and need backup!). One word: cautious. From the friend's point of view, you feel kind of nervous but unsure. You're happy to be with your friend but know nothing about his brother. You're there to give moral support, but the last thing you want to do is cause any trouble. One word: supportive.

Step 3

Now imagine that you are the independent, neutral third-party observer outside of this situation, and see what you perceive. Notice how the behaviors of all parties interact and compare with one another. Notice the overall atmosphere, energy, outcome. Pick one word to describe it.

In this example, you see that a simple miscommunication is unfolding. One brother assumed the meeting would be just the two of them. The other didn't, and brought along a friend for company, not realizing it would create awkwardness. One word: mismatch.

Step 4

Now is the time to reflect. Go back to second position and look again at the facts, seeing if anything has changed. Finish by returning to first position, your perspective, and see if anything has changed there. Is there any new information you possess? New insight?

You can probably already see the value of this perspective switching. If you had merely stayed in first position, you would have dwelt on the inconvenience you felt, and even felt hurt. But by changing positions, you can appreciate that no hurt was intended, and what things look like from both your brother and his friend's point of view. Can you see how this approach will lead you to behave completely differently from the way you might have without switching perspectives?

As you can see, the above technique is a brilliant way to generate real empathy for people and situations and figure out how to really connect and communicate with them. But we can also use this approach when we are trying to more deeply understand the world they live in and their frame of mind within that world—i.e., it's a powerful tool for analyzing people, too.

Let's say you notice your brother bringing along a friend. What does this say about him or the friend? If you can put aside your own perceptual position for a moment, you allow yourself the opportunity to read these actions rather than simply react to them from your own limited position.

Depending on the rest of the context, you may determine a world of information about your brother's discomfort with intimacy, the friendship between him and his friend, and even the friend and his level of conscientiousness or openness. Gradually, you start to develop a working model of other people's personality and position, which are constantly interrelated. It's wonderful to think that, with the right mindset, conflict and misunderstanding are actually nothing more than fascinating data points to feed into the big people-reading machine!

Summary:

- If you can remove bias, expectation, assumption, ego, prejudice, interpretation, and judgment, the better you will be at reading people.
- Distortions and biases (what we think we see) can get in the way of actually seeing. These biases include perceptual selectivity, attribution errors, stereotyping, the halo effect, projection or assuming others are just like us, holding a "perceptual set," using implicit personality theories, expectation, and perceptual defense that causes us to deny or distort what we are seeing if it's perceived as a threat.
- To improve your perceptual accuracy, work hard to know yourself and then cultivate genuine empathy for others; confirm your perceptions are true and compare them against others'; be curious, open-minded, and non-judgmental; ask open-ended questions; and delay forming an opinion about people.
- Perspective taking is the ability to imagine another person's psychological viewpoint—not their life through our eyes, but their life through their eyes. Some ways to

cultivate this skill include trying to understand the perspectives of characters in film and literature. You can also practice switching perspectives to gain insight into conflicts or relationships and understand other people's roles.
- The perceptual positions framework is a basic method for understanding another person's viewpoint. There are three—first, second, and third—and switching between them allows you a richer and more dynamic insight into any situation.
- Personality categories can help us simplify human behavior. One notable theory is the Big Five, or the OCEAN model, which rates people on openness to experience, conscientiousness, extraversion, agreeableness, and neuroticism. Luis Amaral and colleagues have suggested four personality types based on how the Big Five traits usually cluster: "average," "reserved," "self-centered," and "role model."

Section 2

Chapter 4: The Four Functions of Behavior

In the previous chapter, we set about trying to understand what people are like—are they open-minded or more uncurious? Are they "neurotic" or more emotionally even? But what you might notice from this model is that it is not dynamic in any way—it's about what people *are*, not what they *do*.

Especially as outsiders looking in, **we can gain real insights into people's characters by observing their behavior, their choices, and the way they behave.** After all, how do we know that someone is conscientious? We look at their behavior. Someone who merely felt they were conscientious in some vague internal way wouldn't quite make the grade!

In the previous model, we observed behavior and made some inferences about what that means for the person acting that way. For example, we see them talking loudly and animatedly to a big group of people and conclude they are extroverted. In this chapter, we'll consider a model of human behavior that approaches things from the other direction. It asks:

1. How are people behaving?
2. *Why* are they behaving that way (and why do they keep behaving that way)?

This theoretical shift is about seeing personality as a **functional** quality—i.e., as something that we have because it's useful to us in some way. **Understand the function that certain behaviors serve for a person, and you understand who they are**. But before we leap into an explanation of the "four functions," let's take a moment to understand exactly what we're trying to achieve.

Imagine you see a person at a party who is laughing and talking loudly with a big group of people, regaling them with stories. What does it mean? Well, we could say it's proof that the person is outgoing and gregarious, or that they enjoy people. We might get carried away telling ourselves a complicated story about why that person is this way, what it means, and so on . . . but the story may be completely biased. That's because we don't really know what is going on in the head of the person we're observing.

How on earth could we measure their internal state at that moment? We might say "they're extroverted," but the person might actually be acting this way because they're nervous in social situations, and the only way they can reduce that anxiety is to fiercely control the situation—i.e., by dominating socially. They're not extroverts at all; their coping mechanism just makes it look that way!

This explains why some theorists have argued for the use of a "functional behavioral analysis" (FBA) instead of merely telling stories about observed external behavior. **FBA is about formulating a theory about the functional relationship between a person's behavior and their environment**.

It's not about the static, standalone personality traits but about how that person responds to stimuli in their environment. One way to think about this is to imagine a trait like extraversion. Can one stand alone, by themselves, and *be* extroverted? No! Extraversion is something you *do*, and it's a dynamic response to the environment—which in this case also includes other people.

In the previous model, we assumed that people behave the way they do because that's just the way they are. But with this model, people behave the way they do because something in the environment instigates and supports that action. In fact, every time their action is supported this way, it's reinforced—no personality required, just habit!

While personality assessments and profiles might be useful when you're working on your own personal development and self-awareness, it can be tricky when trying to apply to other people because we cannot see into their heads. What we can do, though, is observe the behavior and its environment.

Let's imagine that there are **four functions of behavior**—access, escape, attention, and sensory.

Access – This includes mainly tangible things—items you can literally see and interact with via your five senses.

Attention – This is an interaction, praise, or any kind of feedback or signal from others. This could be anything from a slight increase in awareness and attention from other people to a full-blown reaction from them, or even their subsequent actions and conversations.

Escape – This is about removing an unpleasant item, event, or stimulus from the situation—especially one that has been previously punished and discouraged. An obvious example is the behavior of pulling your hand away from a hot fire. A less obvious example is turning down invitations from people who make you feel bad in subtle ways.

Sensory – This function has no connection to outside factors at all, but rather refers to internal rewards within the body itself. The pleasure of a hug, for example, or the satisfaction of having solved a difficult puzzle.

Furthermore, we can take note of:

1. The antecedent (what comes before the behavior)
2. The behavior (what the behavior is)
3. The consequence or outcome (what the new situation was after the behavior occurred)

Setting things out this way, we can see that behavior can be rewarded or punished, i.e., reinforced or discouraged. Behavior always has an effect on the environment—after all, that's why we do it! Understand all this, and you gain a deeper, functional awareness not just of the person or of the environment, but of their interactive relationship.

All behaviors follow the A-B-C shape, but they will each be maintained by different functions—or a combination of functions. Returning to our example, we can imagine that someone might choose to behave in a gregarious and extroverted way because the behavior serves two broad functions:

1. Escape – taking charge of social situations allows them to escape the anxiety that comes from other people potentially asking intrusive questions, steering the conversation, or making a big deal out of noticing that they are quiet and putting them on the spot.
2. Attention – When this person behaves in this way, people tend to respond in predictable and comfortable ways. The attention they give is a lot easier to deal with than the awkwardness of being asked, "Why are you so quiet?" all the time.

Is the above person extroverted? Yes, in a way. But using functional behavioral analysis allows you to understand the **why** and **how** of the behavior, not merely **what**. Many standup comedians and famous entertainers surprise their fans when they claim to be deeply insecure, private, or introverted individuals. That's because, just as in this example, those fans were only looking at the behavior and not considering what this behavior meant and *why* it was being used.

Let's zoom out and think about how we can use the insights from this kind of behavioral analysis to improve our people-reading skills. The principles are as follows:

- Every action has a reason for happening, so ask yourself what the reward or positive outcome is to see why it's in that person's interest to keep behaving that way. This tells you a lot about them.
- We behave because of how that behavior feels, because of the response we get from our environment, because it gets us something we want, or because it helps us to get away from something we don't want. Try to understand the function of the behavior you're looking at and you will instantly understand it better.
- Personality theories can only go so far. Certain behaviors may be identical in two people who are nevertheless behaving that way for completely different reasons. That's why you

shouldn't consider people in a vacuum or separate their behavior from their environment.

How to Read People Using the ABC Model

Step 1: Identify the behavior

First, just take note of what you're looking at and try to see it without telling any stories about it or making any assumptions—or else self-confirmation bias will creep in. So, instead of noting that "he's extroverted," just note the behavior: "he is talking more loudly and more often than anybody else. He is steering the conversation. He is positioning himself in the center of the group . . ."

Step 2: Collect data to help you establish the antecedent and consequence of this behavior

Now, in our example, if you had never met the person before, you would have much less data to work with. But if you knew them, you could gather plenty of data and combine it with what you know about their behavior at all parties or with other people in general. You could notice how people respond to the loud, excited talking and storytelling. You might notice that the more stressful the situation, the more animated this person becomes. You could even notice that a few years ago, this person was quieter, and people responded to him differently back then.

Step 3: Infer the function of the behavior

Now you put all this data together and make an educated guess about *why* this pattern exists. You could even make a hypothesis and test it. Your hypothesis could be "he behaves in an outgoing and extroverted way so he can cope with and control anxiety-provoking situations." Maybe you decide to test this by seeing how he behaves in less stressful situations, or with smaller groups. You might combine all your guesses with other observations and come to the same conclusion about how the behavior is functioning.

The ABC model is often used by counselors and psychologists to help people get a handle on their own (maladaptive) behaviors. But understanding what triggers and what sustains unwanted behaviors, they give themselves the chance to change things. But you can also use the model in a more open-ended way—**by observing any one of the three components, you can make guesses about the other components, as well as gain insight into the person making those choices.**

Here are a few more common and straightforward examples to show how you can begin using functional behavioral analysis yourself when observing and reading others.

Example 1:

A five-year-old is cheeky and frequently interrupts the adults' conversation.

Antecedent: The adults are not paying her any attention.

Behavior: She does something silly or butts into the conversation.

Consequence: The adults laugh and smile and say things like, "She's such a little character, isn't she?"

Your hypothesis for the function of this behavior: **attention**. The five-year-old reliably wins praise and positive attention from the adults when behaving this way.

Example 2:

Joe is meant to be coming out with you for an early morning run, but instead he's at home in bed, snoozing.

Antecedent: He stayed up late the night before. He's currently in a lovely warm bed.

Behavior: He . . . continues to stay in the lovely warm bed instead of waking up to go run outside in the cold.

Consequence: His running mates are annoyed with him. But also, he gets to stay a few more hours in the lovely warm bed.

Your hypothesis for the function of the behavior: **sensory**. It's not rocket science. Joe is doing what he is doing because it feels good.

Example 3:

Nicky does come along with you on the run that day. In fact, she seems completely jazzed up and ready to go.

Antecedent: Nicky has been having marriage difficulties with Joe, and the two can barely stand to be in the house together these days.

Behavior: She started the running group herself and has worked hard to motivate everyone to the cause.

Consequence: She is grinning from ear to ear after the run, and as soon as it's over, she starts talking about tomorrow's run.

Your hypothesis for the function of the behavior: **escape**. Nicky might want to literally escape her bad marriage, but the running may also serve as a way to escape feelings of frustration, helplessness, and anger, and to give her a sense of purpose when life feels difficult.

If you had only relied on static personality analysis for any of the above examples, you would not have grasped the full situation. That's because it might be the case that the five-year-old is not especially outgoing, Joe is not lazier than average, and Nicky is not a particularly energetic or motivated person, either. Rather, each of their actions is a direct result of their interaction with the environment—and not with their abstract personality or character.

If you've ever found it difficult to read people because they tend *not* to follow patterns, this could be why. **All of us will act against our normal baseline or in ways we're not accustomed to if it serves our purposes in any particular moment.** That's why we need to consider not just the person in front of us or their behavior, but how they and their behavior are embedded into the environment. If we bump into Nicky five years later and she tells us she never kept up her running routine, we won't be too surprised to also hear that she has gotten divorced!

Even in cases where you don't know people well and cannot guess at what came before or what will happen later, you can still get a handle on their behavior by asking what function it serves. Begin by assuming that **people make sense—they behave as they do because, in some way or another, it's working for them**. Yes, even those behaviors that seem completely self-destructive or illogical!

Imagine you have a colleague at work who constantly second-guesses you and checks your work. You do the "perceptual positions" exercise described in the previous chapter, but you're still having a hard time empathizing, and you're beginning to get annoyed. Start by assuming that in his own way, your colleague's behavior makes perfect sense to him, even if not to you. All you have to do is figure out what is triggering that behavior and what is maintaining it. Not only will this give you some insight into what's going on, it might hint at a possible way out of the dynamic once and for all.

Antecedent – You are your colleague's superior, so you're often given more challenging or complex jobs. You also know this colleague would like to advance in their role someday but is new at the company and finding it challenging to distinguish themselves.

Behavior – They stick their nose into your tasks, offering their "help" and "advice" even when it isn't requested.

Consequence – When the task is finished, you typically submit it and get the praise, satisfaction, or reward that comes with it. You also notice that the colleague tends to hover around when you're receiving feedback on these tasks, and once or twice has said, "We did a good job!"

Are you beginning to get a sense of the function of this behavior? It may be a question of **attention**. When behaving this way, your colleague gets to indirectly participate in feelings of having done good work on a job that he does not strictly have access to. This might satisfy a whole host of his needs, such as feeling relevant or convincing himself that he is learning and advancing, even if his actual job title doesn't reflect it.

Two things emerge from this analysis. First, you realize that this colleague must be feeling some sort of insecurity about his position and is perhaps frustrated in his work. Is he struggling to get promoted? Does he not feel recognized in his own tasks, or are they not challenging enough? Second, you start to see a solution to your problem (or a way to test your hypothesis). You simply ask your boss to deliver feedback to you privately. If your theory is correct, the colleague will soon stop the behavior because there will no longer be the same consequence reinforcing it.

Let's say you do receive private feedback... and the behavior continues. Now what? You throw away your hypothesis and make a new one. Could there be a more internal sense of satisfaction that is driving this person (i.e., a sensory function)? Could they perhaps be trying to impress you directly (attention function, but in a different way than you first thought)? Either way, you are closer to understanding their real motivations than if you merely looked at the problem through the "personality type" lens.

Chapter 5: Learning to Read Emotions

Let's change gear once more and consider another rich and nuanced channel of data that we can mine when we observe our fellow humans: emotions.

Nonverbal communication and expression provide us a world of information about a person. What's more, emotion and behavior are linked. Everything we do that's visible is behavior—and that also includes things like facial expressions, gestures, tone of voice, and body posture. Learning to read body language is kind of like learning to read the behavioral component of emotion—our physical attitude in the world is an expression of our internal emotional state.

Now, this may seem like a very obvious point to labor. Is it really so earth-shattering to suggest that people's emotions influence their behavior? Well, yes, when we consider how often we all ignore this kind of information in favor of listening to the words people say, or simply assuming that what they think and feel is more or less the same as what we think and feel. Never underestimate the power of bias and assumption to spoil the most obvious observations!

The great thing about reading body language is that it reveals emotions in a spontaneous, unconscious, and unintentional way—that means you can trust it. And it also means that if what you observe in someone's nonverbal expression differs from what they're communicating verbally, you can read this mismatch itself as a point of interest. It can reveal deception, ambivalence, or a desire to conceal, among other things. Again, context matters; if someone sees something funny during a funeral but does their best to keep a straight face anyway, this is obviously not a question of deception but plain etiquette.

One way to think about body language and emotions is to imagine that human beings only ever express themselves on a single broad continuum, which you can understand loosely as **open or closed**. Broad, expansive gestures suggest confidence, excitement, happiness, trust. Compacted, tight, tense, retreating, and cowering postures suggest disgust, fear, sadness, and so on. Simply being aware of the patterns of relaxation and tenseness in people will already clue you in to the more subtle emotions they may be feeling.

In fact, some theorists (Schutz, 1958) go so far as to suggest that persistent patterns of psychological tension or relaxation actually settle and calcify in the body. So, the person who is constantly angry, critical, or suspicious ends up earning a literal line across their forehead or between their eyes—sustained emotion, in other words, can become a fixed part of the physical body. Think about that next time you see someone who is chronically stooped in posture, has an eternally tight neck and shoulder muscles, or has a face full of smile lines.

Let's take a look at some common behaviors that are expressions not of people's behaviors or personalities, but of how they are feeling in that moment.

Withdrawal, fidgeting, and plenty of small, unnecessary movements suggest **inhibition and anxiety**.

Slow, sparing movements that lack energy and don't seem designed to reach out or connect in any way suggest **depression or exhaustion**.

Fast, expensive, spontaneous, energetic movements and plenty of assertive, confident, and even affected (i.e., almost faked) gestures suggest **elation, joy, self-assuredness**.

Fiddling with hair and skin, wrangling and twisting hands over themselves or holding them in tight fists, or plucking at clothing, eyebrows or objects suggest **stress, repressed anger, or irritation.**

A bent and collapsed body, a slight pout, angled shoulders, and a general vibe of slouching suggests **sadness, defeat, and worry**.

Recoiling slightly, lifting the upper lip, wrinkling the nose, and raising the shoulders suggest **disgust or fear**.

Of course, all of this is relative and context dependent. Wringing your hands and shaking your head at a ball game is totally different from at someone's death bead. One clever trick for reading facial and body expressions is simply to try mimicking the gesture yourself and seeing what emotion it invokes. Try it right now: Gently touch the fingers of both hands to your lips, raise your eyebrows, and let your mouth open a little. What emotion do you feel? If you said "surprise" or even shock or horror, then congratulations, you may be more emotionally literate than you think!

Cultivating "Emotional Granularity"

Pretty much everyone knows that someone who is screaming and holding their hands to either side of their face is probably terrified. But to be masterful at people-reading, you need a little more nuance, i.e., you **need to have a broad and deep knowledge of many different shades of emotion, plus the ability to distinguish between them.**

The trick is that being able to read all the subtleties of emotion in other people requires us to be fairly emotionally literate ourselves. It's about going further than "sadness," and learning to identify the rich palette of emotions that include despair, apathy, misery, resentment, sorrow, grief, disappointment, uneasiness, dismay, anguish, cynicism, or gloom . . .

It's true that some people are simply better equipped to understand emotions, but that absolutely does not mean it's something that can't be learned. What's more, the real skill comes in learning to interpret certain expressions and gestures in context. For example, we saw above that someone behaving in an outgoing and extroverted way doesn't mean that this is simply their personality. Rather, in that example, it was a coping mechanism that served a particular function. Similarly, a smile doesn't always mean happiness, and tears don't always mean sadness. But, noticing these things adds one more data point and, taken together with all your other observations, brings you one step closer to understanding people.

Here are a few ways to train your emotional granularity and expand your emotional vocabulary:

- Read or listen to thought-proving content that uses specific terms to describe feelings. Keep track of your

own responses to various stimuli, both verbal and nonverbal.
- Learn the differences between similar words. You might know that there is a subtle difference but wouldn't know how to pinpoint it when you experience it. One surprising way to do this is to try new and unusual foods. Have you ever noticed how rich the vocabulary is for describing wine? It's the same skill!
- Research words in other languages that could apply to the way you feel right now. By learning new words, you can give your brain more options for predicting and perceiving emotions.
- Think of emotions as occurring on a continuum. If one day you feel, say, bored, try to imagine what that feeling would be if you dialed it up one notch, then another. It might turn into "frustration" or even, at the very high end, something like "resentment." Can you discern the difference all along the scale?
- Make friends with a thesaurus. It seems strange, but looking at synonyms for emotions in a thesaurus can give a finer grasp on the subtle differences. Let's say you're talking to

someone one day, and then pause to try to put a word to their emotion. You choose "pensive." You see that some synonyms include "thoughtful" and "contemplative." This is true, but you also sense a certain distraction in the person. You search around further and settle on different words like "distant" and "detached." Just by fleshing out the various possible adjectives, you're getting a deeper sense of a person's experience—while improving your vocabulary!
- Finally, read fiction and watch movies. Pick a character and challenge yourself to describe how they feel in five words. See if you can track that character's emotions as the story develops.

The Real Way to Read Body Language

Gestures are the body's "emotions."

It makes good sense to look to the body any time you want to understand what someone is feeling. However, most body language advice out there is very one-dimensional. You may see it claimed that if a woman plays with her hair, for example, she is being flirty, or if someone crosses their arms, it means they're standoffish or stubborn.

But if we're using the "X always means Y" approach to reading body language, we won't get very far. The woman may be nervous and distracted; someone may cross their arms because they're cold or trying to hide a stain on their shirt. In other words, it's not that these observations are *wrong*, just that they only really "mean" anything when considered as part of a more complex whole.

You are never merely reading an individual, but reading that individual's behavior and orientation within their environment. A few easy examples: if someone is sitting with their legs sprawled wide on the chair and their belly hanging out, it means two very different things if they behave that way alone in their own living rooms, or on a subway train crowded with people. Looking at your watch when you're standing waiting for the bus means one thing, but a totally different thing when you do it seated at a restaurant with a date. Frowning denotes one thing when you do it during a difficult exam, and another thing when you're listening to someone ask you a big favor. Basically, what a thing ever "means" depends heavily on who is doing it, when, how, and where.

So, just as we considered functional behavior a more illuminating thing to observe than static character traits, let's think about expression and gesture as contextual. Here are a few questions to ask to help you gain more insight into the nonverbal expressions you observe in others.

How does their expression compare to everyone else's?

In a group social setting, notice a person's expression relative to the consensus group expression. Is someone talking much louder than everyone else, adopting a posture much more subdued, dressed in a very different manner, or speaking in a way that doesn't match or mirror those around them? Pay attention to any discrepancies of this kind because they will tell you a lot about what is going on with that person.

Combine your observations with any insights about the function of their behavior. For example, if someone is being way more polite and deferential than everyone else and is smiling a lot more, this may signal an intention to win approval, escape criticism, keep the peace, or else slip beneath the radar. You might confirm this hypothesis if you also see them constantly fretting to offer people drinks or using plenty of defensive and protective body language (for example, shrugging the shoulders as though to lower and hide the self while extending the hands outward, palms open, as though to say "I come in peace!"). By making these observations, you're not only noticing how this person probably feels right now (nervous, vigilant, conciliatory) but also the role they play in this group or in life in general.

Another example: imagine you see a family out and about. Mom, Dad, and two of the children are smiling and laughing, and they have open, relaxed postures and expressions. One child, though, is unsmiling and has tense muscles around their forehead and mouth. This discrepancy tells you that there is something on which this child disagrees with the rest of their family. What is it? Notice what else is going on, and try to find the source of the difference. If the unsmiling child is the eldest teenager, dressed in goth clothing, you can begin to piece together a puzzle about the role this child is presently playing—not to mention the way the other family members are responding to it.

How is their nonverbal expression as a response to stimuli in the environment?

People seldom stand in an empty room and have an emotion. The emotion is almost always in response to something. The way people react to things in their environment tells you a lot about them. Again, it's not rocket science, and we can infer a lot simply by considering the degree of openness or closedness, tension or relaxation.

For example, what can you infer about a person who makes fists and tucks away their hands when someone teases them and puts them on the spot? They are probably not enjoying the challenge/attention. What about when someone leans in to whisper something in another person's ear, and that person responds by touching their neck to pull them in even closer? They are probably feeling (more than) happy with the escalation of intimacy the original gesture symbolized.

"People-watching" is a great way to fine tune this skill. Simply pay attention to people walking, shopping, eating in cafés. Pick someone and see how they respond to other people, to everyday tasks, and so on (politely and unobtrusively, of course!). Try to guess what they are feeling given the way they react to things around them.

You can do this in a smaller, more controlled way every time you converse with someone. Make a small change in the interaction, then watch closely to see how the other person responds to it. For example, touch them lightly on the forearm, change the topic, or ask a slightly more personal question. Then watch for changes in them. For example, if you tell a little joke in which you reveal some harmless but embarrassing detail about yourself, but you notice that the other person remains stoically unchanging in their expression (i.e., they don't laugh, act shocked, or share a similar story of their own), you might guess that they are not interested in the slight escalation of intimacy this move suggests. When you later lean back, adopt a more formal tone, and lessen eye contact, you note they become more relaxed and even start smiling. More evidence for your hypothesis!

How is their nonverbal expression unusual or mismatched?

Often, the most noteworthy aspects of a person's experience are those that are unusual, heightened, or unexpected somehow. Pay attention if someone's responses to something seem (to you, anyway) mismatched. Are they very relaxed in a stressful situation? Smiling whilst getting reprimanded? Look more closely and see what you can infer from this.

People will often respond in overexaggerated ways when the matter is something they are ashamed, confused, or angry about. Defensiveness in general suggests a lack of confidence or feeling of vulnerability. On the other hand, people who seem to show too little emotion may communicate loud and clear all the same.

Imagine that you notice that someone is getting extremely flustered and stressed while trying to save a phone number on their mobile phone. You watch them and notice that they get irritable and clumsy, and then almost give up when their first attempt doesn't work. They're blushing, almost angry. Considering other observations (they are an older person, unfashionably dressed, retired, and soft-spoken), you assume that this total overreaction to the annoyances of technology says something about their discomfort and resentment of modern life.

Perhaps they are embarrassed by their lack of ability, or perhaps you can infer that they have never bothered with certain material trappings because they prioritize other values. Perhaps their reaction tells you something about their attitude toward *you*—do they worry you will think they're just a foolish old person and will get annoyed and impatient with them? Whatever it is, this little detail about the phone is a gem and can help you build a rich and nuanced picture of the person in front of you.

You can also stay alert not just to over- or under-reactions, but to reactions that just seem odd, unusual, or unexpected. For example, you may be with someone when you both experience a sudden frightening situation—let's say an attempted mugging or a mild earthquake. You notice that not only is the other person *not* frightened, but they seem to actually be enjoying it! What could this tell you?

You might conclude that this person is a thrill seeker, a little bored in their own life, or even that their tolerance of risk, danger, and novelty is unusually high. On the other hand, if the person leaves the situation completely distraught and talking nonstop about what *they* experienced and how traumatized *they* are, you can guess they are pretty self-focused or like to imagine themselves as victims!

Why You Can't Always Trust Facial Expressions

Way back in 1972, with the publication of *The Expressions of the Emotions in Man and Animals*, Darwin first suggested that human emotions map onto distinct facial expressions. The trouble with humans, though, is that we may be in situations where we wish to conceal our emotions, or else appear to be feeling ones we aren't.

Richard Restak is the author of *Mozart's Brain and the Fighter Pilot: Unleashing Your Brain's Potential*, and he provides a simple exercise designed to improve your ability to read other people's emotions. Restak claims that "when a person pretends an emotion, he or she activates the same brain areas that would be activated in circumstances when the emotions are naturally and spontaneously expressed."

Try this exercise. Get a trusted friend and position yourself around three feet away from one another. Get your friend to close their eyes. Gaze at your friend's face and ask them to think about the saddest memory they have of their life, but also instruct them that they shouldn't respond in any way—for example, by sighing or frowning. Watch their face and see if you can note any subtle changes.

Next, ask your friend to completely clear their mind and think of nothing. Again, watch and see what you can see. Now ask your friend to open their eyes and look at you, again thinking about the saddest moment in their life, followed by a completely neutral experience, say, buying milk at the store. Finally, ask the friend to imagine the happiest moment of their lives. Throughout, keep a close watch on their face, especially the eyes. In particular, notice what happens in the moments when one emotion *shifts* to another.

The exercise is also illuminating when you switch roles. What did you both notice? Is there anything you're especially surprised by?

You may find that what your friend tells you they were thinking about and what you perceived in their facial expression were totally at odds. For example, from your perspective, they might have seemed totally serene and confident, but they tell you they were at that moment recalling the distressing moment they learned their grandmother had died. You'll notice this the other way around, too, and be surprised at how badly wrong your friend read your expressions. Sure, in hindsight you may be able to read certain subtleties in an entirely different way. But what if you were *only* relying on your reading of their facial expression?

The point of this exercise is not to show you that facial expressions are meaningless and that it's not worth paying attention to them. Rather, **it's to show just how hidden people's true emotions can actually be.** The exercise shows you how well people can conceal their actual emotions, even when you think you may be seeing something in the movement of an eyebrow or the twitch of a lip.

Something else you might notice is that the transitions themselves provide more information than any single facial movement or gesture. In other words, what you might be discerning is the *effort* someone is making to conceal their emotions, or else the change from one emotion to another. Even if someone is doing their best to hide their true feelings, you can still infer something when a stimulus gets some kind of rise out of them. What does it mean? Well, the rest of the context and all your other observations will help you find the answer.

Consider this example. You're having a disagreement with a family member because you strongly suspect them of lying to you. Let's say you're having a discussion, and their facial features are lively and animated. Then you bring up the issue of the lie, and this suddenly changes. Their face goes blank. They start making simple, clear, concise statements and repeating themselves. What does their facial expression tell you? Well, nothing. But the sudden change from expressive to non-expressive tells a big story. Even though the topic is distressing and you're unhappy, they don't mirror this or respond in a normal way to it.

What you are noticing is actually the lack of expression or, more accurately, the effort being made to create that impression. What does it mean? There is an attempt to minimize or hide something, or else to de-escalate the situation. This person may not be outright lying to you, but they are definitely trying to avoid showing you *something*. We will explore this issue of lie detection in a later chapter, but first, we need to consider a very important concept in the art of people-reading.

Chapter 6: Baselining

Picture this. You meet someone new for the first time, and they are grinning ear to ear. They immediately start gushing about how much they love your shoes, and when you start talking, they listen with rapt attention, laughing (loudly) at all your jokes and telling you afterward that they have never met anyone quite so interesting as you. When you part ways, they make a big deal about getting your contact details and invite you to their house, but not before giving you an enormous hug to say goodbye.

What do you think about such a person? You probably assume that they really, really like you. They seem ultra-friendly and positive and like they really enjoyed your company. Maybe other observations make you think that they might be a bit lonely and hungry for company, or even that they're coming onto you. That is, until you meet this person again, this time in a group. You see that they treat *everyone* this way. You suddenly realize that they don't think you're especially great—that's just what they're like with everyone!

The behavior, in a vacuum, usually does indicate someone who is interested, positive, happy, etc. But these in-a-vacuum observations don't tell you how common this behavior is *compared to that person's own tendencies.* Perhaps, after watching them interact with other people for a while, you actually realize that they are a little less warm and friendly to you than they normally are in general.

It's important to consider any single behavior not just as it compares to other people or to the environment itself, but to the person behaving that way. In other words, is this behavior common or uncommon *for them*?

We can't make any conclusions about the information we gather if we don't have something to compare it to. What seems normal to you might not be normal to them, and so on. **A baseline is a set of nonverbal**

behaviors (like posture, movement, and gestures) that a person usually uses when they are comfortable and relaxed. It's like a default setting.

When you read body language, you are looking at expression in absolute terms, but also relative terms. You decide whether something is noteworthy according to how far from the baseline it is. If the person above meets someone and you observe them being polite and kind, but very much less so than normal, you can probably conclude they don't like that person—even if their behavior is objectively friendlier than the average.

Body language experts agree that you should pay attention to the subtleties and *changes* in a person's body language to know when it's been activated or triggered during a normal conversation. Notice all the ways in which they are behaving differently from what's normal for them.

The first step, if you can, is to establish a baseline. Here are things to look for:

- Blink rate
- Eye contact—how frequent and duration

- Breathing—both rate and depth
- Body movement speed and fluidity
- Facial expressions
- Gestures used
- Cadence, pitch, volume, articulation, and rhythm of voice
- Overall posture—open or closed, tense or relaxed

Note, of course, that the above all need to be considered **in context**. So, someone's baseline when they are at work doing their teaching job may be completely different from their baseline on the weekend when they're with friends and doing a hobby.

It's difficult to establish a baseline for someone the first time you meet—you will typically need to spend more time with them in different contexts to begin to notice any stable patterns. That said, you can still use the principle of baselining even if you only engage with a person for a short time. For example, during the course of a twenty-minute conversation, you might establish a baseline *for that conversation*, and this allows you to detect when something suddenly changes. In fact, being aware of how people change over the course of a single interaction is also what will allow you to gracefully end the conversation at the right time.

Using Baselines to Detect Deception

The baseline approach is especially useful for one type of people-reading: catching liars.

Many people believe all sorts of myths about how you can catch a liar red-handed (they look up and to the left, they bite their lip, etc.), but these will seldom help you. **A better way to find out if someone is lying is to identify "leakage," which is unintentional and inconsistent communication across multiple channels like:**

- Facial expressions
- Gestures and body language
- Voice
- Communication style
- Verbal statements

A leak can be anything—but it is always something different from the baseline, something that was intended to be concealed but wasn't. Spot it, and you can infer a bigger concealment that may be underway. Let's take a look at how this may play out in real life.

Step 1: Gather information

Everyone has a "norm," which is a basic preferred setting for how they act when they are under normal amounts of stress. This can be anything from how often or quickly they blink, to the words they usually use. A person often has a "tic," or a sign that they are uncomfortable, just like they have a "norm." You've seen these expressions on your family and friends: a quick smirk or frown when you say something they don't agree with, or a tendency to suddenly muddle words. But even if you see a "tic," keep looking. A tic doesn't automatically mean a lie. But it does tell you something—what you continue to observe will help clarify what that something is.

Try to answer the questions:

What is normal for this person?
How does this change when they are experiencing stress?
When and where are the most dramatic differences?

You may gather this information all at once in a single conversation, or you may need to really get to know a person well first.

Step 2: Establish rapport

Now, if you were an FBI agent trying to uncover deception, you might need to quickly establish rapport to build on. Since you're probably not an FBI agent, just apply this step in whatever way suits your situation. It goes without saying that if you have just met someone or don't know them well, your chances of finding out the truth will be greater if you can establish some kind of shared understanding and connection with them first. This will put them at ease (without stress, you can more easily establish their baseline) and also put you at ease, making you more observant.

Even if you already have an established relationship with the person, the way that you talk to them will make a big difference to how they communicate with you. Of course, at no point should you give any hint that you are trying to uncover deception. Be relaxed, make eye contact but not too much, be warm and steady, and invite them to tell their stories by listening with relaxed and respectful empathy. If you are unguarded, they will be too. Ask open-ended questions rather than leading immediately by grilling them with what you want to know, and don't come across as too forceful or determined. One good way to subtly promote rapport is to mirror them in small ways—adopt the same posture, tone of voice, expression, or even verbal idiosyncrasies to show that you're on the same wavelength.

Step 3: Run through the baseline checklist

The following five-part checklist is about making as thorough an observation as possible, in as short a time period as you can. While you're making your observations, though, remind yourself that what you don't observe can be as important as what you do! The general rule is to start your way at the top of the person and work your way down:

1. First, observe the face

- What is the position of their head and how are they holding it?
- Are they touching their face? How and where? How often?

- Watch the eyes—where are they looking? How fast are they blinking?
- Can you notice any tension or looseness in the mouth?

2. Next, listen to the voice

- What is the tone or character of the voice? Smooth, jerky, wavering, clear, monotone?
- Is the pitch low, medium, or high?
- Listen for both kinds of volume—loud or soft, but also how much talking they're doing.
- How fast or slow are they talking? Is their pace consistent or all over the place?

3. Listen to the words they're saying

- Do they use verbal fillers (um, ah, like)? How often?
- Are they being formal or causal? Swearing?
- Do they use full sentences? Are the sentences unusually long or short?
- How is their grammar? For example, do they frame things in passive voice or state everything as a question?
- Do they use a lot of "I" and "me"?

4. Notice how they're holding their body

- How much space are they taking up? Are they spreading out or collapsing? Rigid or yielding?
- Is their posture generally open or more closed? Tight or loose?
- Do they seem to be advancing or retreating?
- Notice their gestures—are they wide and expansive or small, nervous, and useless?

5. Finally, take note of the fidget factor

- Are there lots of unnecessary and pointless gestures? What kind?
- What do they do in a relaxed position?
- Is their overall impression one of movement or stillness? Calm or agitation?

Okay, great. Now that you've gathered all this data, what do you do with it?

Your main goal as a deception-detector is to look for stress signals that alert you to an inner state of effort, anxiety, or dissonance.

What does this mean? Think about what it's like to lie. If your brain is a computer, then lying represents an additional computational burden that asks your brain to work far harder than it would have to if it was just recounting the truth. In the same way that a CPU that is hard at work will sometimes make loud noises or start to get hot, you can learn to look for the human "stress signals" that tell you that some additional work is underway—potentially a lie.

Right away, you can see the first problem with using this approach—i.e., someone may be burdened with extra thinking not because they're lying but because they're unhappy for another reason, or simply nervous (perhaps because they sense you're interrogating them!). Again, the only way out of this dilemma is to continually observe the whole and consider what you're observing, even making allowances for the fact that someone might be nervous for some other reason.

You always want to take into account:

Social norms
The impact of the context and environment

The social role that person is currently playing
What they may be trying to achieve with their behavior in general
The nature of your relationship
Their normal personal baseline
Any other potential sources of stress
The unique way their expression changes in response to stress

Once you've gathered information and established a baseline, your next move is to **watch very closely for anything that does not fit that baseline.** The logic is that if you are familiar with how a person behaves when relaxed, then you can clearly notice when they are stressed and outside that range—i.e., might be telling a lie. That's why every attempt to uncover an untruth always begins with establishing a connection, rather than jumping in with accusations, threats, or targeted questions—these will naturally just make the person clam up. Even worse, when they start behaving in a stressed way, you won't know if this is because they're genuinely lying, or just because it's stressful to be accused this way!

Once you have established rapport and observed them in their relaxed and calm state, and you pose a meaningful question, *then* their sudden change in behavior will tell you something useful. Though you don't need to practice this skill in the way that professional interrogators do, the principles are actually the same. Let's look at an example.

Let's say you are interviewing a candidate for a role in your company, but you have reason to believe they're not being especially truthful on their resume. Now, you're not too concerned about the white lie—it's rather small—but you are concerned about the overall trustworthiness of the candidate and bluntly want to see how good they are at hiding the truth! Either way, you will learn something interesting about them.

You begin with two simple questions: What's normal for this person? How do they behave when they're stressed out?

You prepare for the interview by reading up on them as much as you can beforehand, and try to make inferences based on their age, where they grew up, education, social media use, background, etc. This can only take you so far, though. You look at the way they've compiled their resume. You see what they are emphasizing (their degree and awards) and what is de-emphasized or not mentioned at all (a gap of two years, their exact job title at a previous position, etc.). This tells you a lot about how this person wants to present themselves. What *aren't* they showing, and why?

In the interview, you simply begin by getting to know them. You keep things very warm and relaxed and even make out that you're not a seasoned interviewer and don't intend to take the process all that seriously. You do what you can to put them at ease—smiling, eye contact, offering to make them a coffee, leaning in close, and making friendly small talk about relatable things.

But all the while this is happening, you are watching them. You are paying attention to those five areas of observation to establish the baseline. Now, you already know that an interview is a naturally stressful situation, so all you are doing is looking for what the baseline level of stress is before the "real interview" begins. You notice:

Lots of eye contact and smiling
Leaning forward in the chair
Voice medium loud, strong, even

Fidgety hands
Lots of "I" statements
Lots of nodding along
Tight but active overall posture; impression of alertness and energy

Great. So this is what the candidate looks like under the normal conditions of interview stress. Once you're sure that rapport has been established and you have a baseline (i.e., run through the five-point checklist in your head), then you can start pressing on what you believe to be the deception. You first ask about something that you know is true, and observe the response.

"So you went to Harvard."
"Yeah, I did."
"This was in . . . 2019? Okay, so I also see you took an extra year to complete your degree."
"Yeah, that's right. I was in quite a bad car crash and so I graduated a little later."
"I'm sorry to hear that. But it says here that you went straight from that into your position with the first startup, is that right?"
"Yeah, that's correct. Spring of 2020, I began work with *Real Time*."

While on the surface all this seems pretty run-of-the-mill, you are actually hard at work noticing the way the candidate responds to questions when it's the truth: short, to-the-point answers, frequently beginning with "yeah" and accompanied by an energetic nod, eye contact, and an alert posture. **This is what the truth looks like for this person in this context.** Let's move on.

"Well, we've been looking for developers like you for ages, so it would be great to have you on board. But I'm curious, it seems like your last role would have been more your speed, salary-wise at least. Why the change?" Now, you play it cool and watch. You notice these things:

The candidate keeps smiling and making eye contact, but all at once, they lean back in the chair and fold their hands firmly in their lap. Their voice drops in volume and pitch, and their posture seems to spread and loosen a little.

"There are a lot of reasons for that, the primary one being issues with their initial stages of funding. The company was bought out, but there was a lack of overall interest from investors. Long story short, I'm looking for a little more security regarding pay."

What to make of this answer? Let's say that you happen to *know* that this is a white lie. You know the founders of *Real Time* and know that although financing was tight at first, this particular employee was fired for completely unrelated reasons. It's not a big deal, but you make a note of this. **This is what this person looks like when they're lying**—or at least bending the truth! Let's move on again.

You ask them some more questions, keep them at ease, and then you finally ask the question you are most interested in.
"If we offered you this role, do you see yourself remaining on for the foreseeable future? At this stage, we are really looking ahead at the long term, and we want to start bringing in people who can grow with us. Does that align with what you're after?"

Let's say the candidate does this: They lean back even further and give another formal, long-winded answer, some of it in passive voice and delivered in a kind of low-energy way compared to their previous answers. They assure you they are very committed to the role. You ask some further questions, and their demeanor changes again, back to what you have already registered as the baseline.

So, does this mean they were lying about wanting to stay in the role for the long term? It's not *conclusive* . . . but the evidence strongly suggests it! Crucially, if you had simply followed ordinary body language (i.e., fidgeting and nervous, tight posture equals lying), then you would have completely gotten this wrong. You would have assumed that the calm, relaxed-looking person who was speaking clearly and articulately was telling the truth. But for this person, whose natural state was more energetic and excitable, this relaxed body language was, ironically, a "stress signal" hinting at deception.

As you can imagine, learning to spot liars is more like a dark art that requires years of practice to master. At first, try not to think of it as "catching a liar." Rather, just become aware of people's patterns and shifting energies in any interaction or conversation. Become good at noticing changes and shifts. Learn to see the switch from normal to unusual. Yes, this will help you become better at spotting lies, but it will more generally help you become a brilliant people-reader.

Chapter 7: Watch Wardrobe, Walk, and Food

"The clothes maketh the man," says the old proverb. It turns out that not only does a person's wardrobe tell you a lot about them, but so does the way they walk, the shoes they wear, and what and how they eat. However, all the same rules about perception and non-verbal expression apply, and we need to learn to regard people with genuinely fresh eyes.

Clothing Speaks

Jennifer Baumgartner, a clinical psychologist and author, has always been interested in the "psychology of dress." In her fascinating book, *You Are What You Wear: What Your Clothes Say About You*, she explores this complex relationship: not only how **psychology affects our clothing choices, but also how our clothing choices in turn can impact our psychology**. On a personal level, understanding how you are portraying yourself aesthetically is, she claims, as important as understanding your biases, beliefs, and communication style—in fact, clothing *is* a communication style!

Northwestern University recently explored the concept they called "enclothed cognition" in a study. In their report, researchers define it as "the systematic effect that clothes have on the psychological processes of the wearer." This means what your clothes say to you, not about you, and how you feel about them. But for our purposes as budding people-readers, we can see that clothing is also a brilliant window into a person's current state of mind. Let's imagine that we are extending our understanding of body language (gesture, voice, posture, facial expression) to include the choices a person makes every time they get dressed in the morning—let's call it fine-tuning our "enclothed perception."

Both Baumgartner and the researchers at Northwestern University would suggest that you don't dress based on how you feel, but based on how you *want* to feel. Want to feel strong, sexy, serious, in control, or relaxed? Then dress that way. However, we are also interested in the fact that people do tend to pick clothing that mirrors their emotional state. Look at the clothes and you see the emotion.

As you can guess, however, there are some caveats (and they're not that different from the caveats we keep in mind when reading body language in general).

- Context matters—if people have to wear something as a part of their job or social role, it implies much less about them, for example.
- Age, gender, ethnicity, social class, and background all play a role too—what is considered daring for one group may be conservative for another. What is expensive-looking in one country may be casual in another.
- Historical period—obviously, our shared cultural understanding of what the vocabulary of fashion means will change over time!

Baumgartner also explains how it's not just the clothing itself, but the way a person wears that clothing. The messages are quite obvious when you stop to pay close attention to them. For example:

A person who keeps everything they own, never throwing anything away, or else a person who is still wearing things from decades prior may be clinging to the past.

A person who wears neutrals only, "basics," and no accessories may be stuck in a rut, too comfortable, complacent.

A person wearing clothing that's too big for them may have yet to update to a smaller body size from their past, or they might desire to hide something.

Someone who consistently dresses to emphasize sex appeal is very culture dependent, but likely either craves attention from the opposite sex and envisions their identity primarily in these terms, or else they are insecure in this area and are trying to encourage others to see them this way. Occasionally, this style can suggest that a person is playing what they feel is the role they've been assigned.

Dressing too "young" or too "old" hints at the age that the person feels themselves to be, or either what they wish to convey to others. This style may point to signals around maturity, sex appeal, professionalism, or class.

A person who basically only wears work clothes—obviously, their "uniform" tells you the role they are most commonly inhabiting. Whether in a good or bad way, work is a big part of their identity.

A person who is always wearing designer logos or expensive status markers wants you to treat them well. They want to be seen as winners or in a special category above others. They may be very goal driven and seek external validation and approval, basing their aspirations on conventional symbols of wealth and prestige.

The person forever in jeans/tights and a relaxed hoodie or sweatshirt—unless they are literally coming back from the gym or a walk, assume this person has put their own vanity on the back burner and is focusing on something else, such as parenthood. It may signal low self-worth, exhaustion, or a lack of purpose.

A person deliberately wearing a symbol that connects them to a certain group—be it a band T-shirt, a religious necklace, a hat with a political slogan, or a tattoo of a meme—sees themselves as one of the group, but also that they wish for others to recognize that fact.

Just as we do with every other behavioral observation, we need to interpret clothing **in context**. For example, you might have met someone wearing a torn T blouse with shoulder pads, a tulle skirt, high top sneakers, and a crocheted handbag made out of seashells. Her hair was full of untidy clips and bows, and she was wearing bright-red lipstick and horn-rimmed glasses.

Now, if the woman were eighty years old and wearing all this to her granddaughter's graduation, we might think that her choices signaled a kind of nostalgia, lack of connection to current trends, or else an endearing disregard for other people's opinions. But if the woman were twenty-three years old and wearing this to a job interview, we would conclude something entirely different. We might wonder why she was so eager to communicate that she was different from the norm. Was she a very dramatic person? Insecure? Flamboyant? Genuinely unconventional and artistic? A bit self-absorbed? Your other observations will help you decide.

As with other body language, it's worth watching for changes from the baseline, or clothing that is out of sync with others, unexpected, or exaggerated in some way. If you have gone on several dates with a person, every time with them turning up super well-dressed and groomed, ask yourself what it means if they show up to date number seven wearing tracksuit bottoms and an old gym shirt. They may suddenly be feeling more comfortable around you, or else they have unofficially abandoned "the chase" and decided that, for whatever reason, it was no longer necessary to impress you.

It's not just clothing. A 2012 study investigated how well people are able to make character judgments about others just by looking at the shoes they wear most of the time. They concluded that a snapshot of a person's favorite footwear *can* reveal a lot about them, including their age, income, and even attachment anxiety. On their own, shoes reveal a tiny amount of information about the wearer, but this information can be quite useful. According to Gillath et al., shoes are a pretty accurate thing to look at for good first impressions. Consider:

Flat shoes indicate a humble person who gets things done without requiring supervision or praise.

High heels can signal confidence, deliberation, ambition, and perhaps a need for attention.

Flashy shoes can, naturally, hint that a person is an extrovert and likes to stand out.

Flip flops point to a relaxed, easygoing attitude that may tend to laziness.

Shoes that are always squeaky clean and polished suggest the desire to make a good first impression and someone who takes care of their life and themselves.

High-healed black ankle boots or "Chelsea" boots may suggest confidence or even aggression. Often worn by people who know *exactly* what they want in life. On the other hand, tan or brown cowboy-style ankle boots are typically worn by more relaxed, arty types.

Shoes that are in poor repair or constantly dirty may suggest this person doesn't take care of themselves, either.

Formal lace-ups or expensive loafers, especially if not in a professional context, are somber-looking "classic" shoes that suggest someone wants to be taken seriously and that they value tact, discipline, and order.

Sports shoes could symbolize being goal-oriented and active, but if they're more like ordinary sneakers or street shoes, the person may be versatile and energetic and find it easy to get along with everyone. On the other hand, if those sneakers cost two hundred dollars, then the story they tell is a little different...

"Sensible" footwear suggests that people are secure in themselves and internally motivated. Birkenstocks, for example, suggest someone loves comfort, the outdoors, and quality things—and that they prioritize comfort over style.

Barefoot—well! Depending on the context, you could be dealing with a rugged outdoor type, a dedicated rebel, or a toddler...

Naturally, shoe choices will take on different meanings depending on time and place. In some parts of the world, at some points in history, red shoes were associated with prostitutes. Of course, if you saw red shoes on the pope (a centuries-old papal fashion), you would not make that association! That's why observing shoe type is not enough on its own. Notice how people take care of their shoes—or not. Do they insist on wearing light-colored or delicate shoes that require constant cleaning? See if you can notice signs of perfectionism, competitiveness, or obsessiveness in the rest of their behavior.

Do they regularly toss their shoes to the side when they take them off, allow them to get dirty and broken, walk freely through dirt and water, or insist on wearing shoes that are ugly, inappropriate, or ill-fitting? Look for other signs of either a free spirit or a general air of self-negligence. Do they constantly wear shoes that do not match the occasion? Become curious about what they value instead. Do they prioritize fashion over conformity or comfort? Would they rather be cold than ugly?

Remember, though, that you need to think about the type of shoes that people wear most often. Consider also that a person who has an enormous wardrobe of very different shoes may value novelty and choice more than a person who literally wears the same pair every single day. Finally, shoes have a way of telling you about the person someone wishes they could be. If you can, peek into someone's closet and notice if there's a difference between what the person wears everyday and what they tend to buy again and again. A woman who lives in worn-out ballet flats but keeps on buying sparkly stilettos is telling you something about how she sees herself—and what she is aspiring to. It's a point worth bearing in mind: not everyone sees themselves accurately!

It's in the Way You Walk

Werner Wolff, a German-born psychologist, did one of the first studies examining the connection between gait (the way people walk) and personality. How a person walks, including their speed and stride length, can speak volumes. Everyone is different, and so is the way they walk. It's even been suggested that the way a person walks can give clues about what they are trying to hide from the world. Again, none of this is rocket science, but it does require us to pause and pay attention and carefully analyze what we are observing.

If someone is a fast walker, they may be a hardworking, outgoing person. Fast walkers tend to be open-minded, extroverted, and conscientious. Go-getters and risk-takers walk fast. They will be bolder than usual, energetic, and detail-oriented. They may also be more stressed!

If someone walks slowly and takes short steps, it's more likely they're an introvert. People who have a slow-walker personality tend to turn inward more often, are more contemplative, and keep to themselves. Most of the time, people who walk this way are calm and happy when they are by themselves. When there are a lot of people in a room, you might notice them move into the background or away from the center of attention.

If someone's walking style is loose and relaxed, it shows that they like to live life on their own terms and at their own speed. They're not in a hurry to be anywhere but here and now. They're also not in a hurry to take orders. They're calm, happy, and sure of themselves inside and out, but won't fight for the spotlight or stay ahead of the crowd.

If someone usually takes long, quick strides, they probably have a healthy attitude about life. Covering a lot of ground when walking suggests competitiveness, focus, and a desire to get things done. People still like them even if they sometimes come off as a little cold.

If someone is always dragging their feet, it suggests an anxious personality prone to worry. People who walk this way are usually upset or sad. They can't pull away from things or thoughts that make them feel bad. They can't stay in the present moment very often. They keep dragging around their past or worry about losing things or people they care about.

But once again, context and baseline make all the difference. Notice how a person is walking *relative to* others in group or compared to how they normally walk. Notice if they always want to walk side by side with others, dawdle, or want to be in front. As with other body language, look for the openness or closedness of the body, look for dynamism (suggesting confidence, joy, etc.) and gesture. **One way to think of walking is that it is like a visual representation of the way a person thinks**. Describe their walk and you have described their cognitive processes. Are they confident, relaxed, and easy thinkers? Are they always going somewhere rather than just stretching their legs? Are they walking like a queen or scuttling nervously along like a crab?

Observe a Person's Food Choices

Juliet Boghossian is a food behavior expert in Los Angeles and founder of the food behavior research firm Food-ology. According to her, a person's eating habits can tell you enormous amounts about their personality, priorities, values, and identity. And why wouldn't it be that way, considering that what and how we eat probably represents dozens of choices we each make every day?

Observe people's behavior around food and drink and you can infer a lot about their state of mind and the way they think of themselves and the world. According to Boghossian:

If someone eats slowly, they tend to like to be in charge, and they know how to savor life. They are also usually sure of themselves, in control, and calm.

If someone eats quickly, they tend to be ambitious, goal-oriented, and open to new experiences, but they may also have a tendency to be impatient. Eating quickly can also suggests distraction and anxiety, so watch for other context clues.

If someone loves to try new food, then you can safely assume that they are open-minded and curious types, and they may be a lot less judgmental than the average person. This willingness to move out of a comfort zone can signal creativity, maturity, a joyful disposition, or perhaps a tendency toward boredom.

If someone is picky about what they eat, it generally suggests discomfort and anxiety of some kind or other. It's no coincidence that picky eating is most commonly associated with children, who are still developing their sense of discipline, adventurousness, and trust in the world. A fussy eater may demonstrate fearfulness or lack of maturity in other areas of life, or they may be signaling a pronounced desire to control the external environment in an attempt to moderate themselves internally.

On the other hand, a limited palette can also be a simple question of habit and background. So much of what we enjoy eating comes down to how we have been raised, our culture, our income, what is available to us, and what brings us the most joy. What can you infer about an adult who won't eat their vegetables or who only ever wants to eat cheese pizza? It could be poor discipline, bad habit, or a more serious aversion . . . or all of these. Gather more data and you will get a clearer picture!

If someone likes to eat one food at a time, they are the so-called "isolationists." These people eat all of one food before moving on to the next, and so on around the plate. They pay a lot of attention to details and always give things a lot of thought. Predictably, they may like to do only one task at a time. They may be conscientious, a little anxious, disciplined, but possibly "control freaks" who would prefer if life stayed neat and orderly.

As you're making your observations, become curious about *everything* you see:

- How are their table manners? Slurping and talking with their mouth full, or taking pains to be neat and delicate?
- Are they comfortable eating in front of others?
- Are they very certain about their preferences, or do they find making a decision difficult?
- Do they order the same thing everyone else does?

- Do they order the cheapest or most expensive thing on the menu?
- Do they avoid complaining if given the wrong food?
- How do they treat the waiter?
- Do they offer to pay, or do they wait coyly for you to do it?
- Are they snobby and disparaging about the food?
- Are they consciously dieting and talking about food in combative terms?
- Do they whip out their phone for Instagram pics while their food gets cold?
- Do they take food off your plate, offer you a taste of theirs, or happily chat to the people at the next table?

As you can see, it's all grist for the people-reading mill. Perhaps now you can see the wisdom of businesspeople inviting one another out to lunch for meetings. It's not a social occasion, but an opportunity to mine the rich data that comes from observing people doing ordinary things like wear clothes, walk, and eat. In just a ten-minute snack break, you can observe:

How a person walks

Their voice—pace, pitch, timbre, volume, etc.
Their body language and facial expression
Their clothing choice
Their posture, gestures, and way they move
The language they employ
The literal words they say

It's a lot of information, but all this data really starts to mean something when it's put all together and embedded properly in the environment from which it emerged. Importantly, when making your observations, try to keep your own assumptions and values out of the picture. **What you are trying to understand is what a certain food behavior means to them, not to you.** They may tell you that they are a vegetarian, and you maya assume this is because they care about animal welfare, and then start telling yourself a story about how compassionate and conscientious they are. In fact, they are vegetarian for the health benefits only, and primarily because it's doctor's orders—that paints a very different picture!

A big caveat here: humans are judgmental. Yes, even us! At any one time there is a whole world of signs and symbols out there, most of them attached to a "good" or "bad" label. But it's only when we drop this value judgment and become genuinely curious that we can start to understand what we're actually looking at. The deeper you go, the more thorough your understanding. If you are lazy and simply think, "That guy makes tea in the microwave. I bet he's some kind of psychopath," then you are missing out on a whole universe of valuable information.

Summary:

- We can gain real insights into people's characters by observing their behavior, their choices, and the way they behave, plus the function of this behavior. Functional behavioral analysis is about formulating a theory about the functional relationship between a person's behavior and their environment, and not just static personality traits. Their behavior function may be access, attention, escape, or sensory. We can also observe the antecedents and consequences of behavior to see what triggers and sustains it.
- Nonverbal communication provides us a world of information about a person, and emotion and behavior are

linked. Body language reveals emotions in a spontaneous, unconscious, and unintentional way. Don't just read an individual, but that individual's behavior and orientation within their environment. Look for unusual, mismatched expressions and how people respond to those around them.

- Develop emotional granularity, which is a broad and deep knowledge of many different shades of emotion, plus the ability to distinguish between them. Remember that emotions can be concealed; watching for transitions and responses may be more illuminating.
- A baseline is a set of nonverbal behaviors that a person shows when relaxed. Pay attention to different-for-them behavior and consider context. Baselining can also help you identify lies and deception. Establish a baseline when relaxed, add stress and observe, then ask the relevant question and watch what happens.
- Finally, consider clothing, shoes, gait, and food choices as an extension of body language. The way a person walks can tell you about how they

think and their level of ambition and stress, clothing can signal identity and intention, and food choices tell you a lot about a person's values and background.

Section 3

Chapter 8: NLP and People's Meta-Programming

In NLP, or neurolinguistic programming, **meta-programs are basically our "maps of reality."** These maps describe our style of thinking, feeling, sorting, valuing, and choosing information and perceptions, and consequently they affect how we behave. It can be fascinating to learn more about your own mental models of the world, but meta-programs can also offer us a rich insight into how *other* people tick.

So how do meta-programs work?

Whenever a person encounters something in the world, they form an internal representation of that event (i.e., a program) within their own minds. *How* they do this depends very much on a larger organizing principle, i.e., their meta-programs. The brain is a pattern-making machine and loves to make shortcuts and models of what it experiences. But the key is that brains are completely unique in the patterns they see (and don't see!), the meaning they make, the things they find most important, and the shortcuts they create.

Luckily, these internal models, though invisible, reveal themselves in countless ways as a person interfaces with other people and the world at large. **To fully understand someone's meta-program, we need only pay attention to their words, body language, and actions**—these are reflections of the kind of mental representation that person is working with.

For a quick example, imagine that you are riding a rollercoaster with three new friends. As you round the corner, you are surprised by a scary fake monster that jumps out at you. Everyone screams (you included), but you notice with interest that their reactions beyond this are quite different. One friend then immediately breaks out into laughter, a second friend gets a little angry and defensive, and the third starts mocking and teasing the second for being a big baby.

It's a small observation, but this difference in the way your new friends react to *the same stimulus* can tell you a lot about the internal mental maps they are working from. You notice how they talk about this moment the next day. The first friend talks about the group and how much fun "we" had and how everyone enjoyed themselves. The second friend complains about the surprise being sprung on them with no warning and talks at length about how unfair it is and how doubly unfair it is that the third friend is being mean to them. The third friend says how they can't wait to go back to test to see if it's as scary the second time round.

These differences in reaction are interesting because they reveal something about the hidden worldviews from which they sprang. The first friend is showing you that they think of the world as a largely happy, non-threatening place, but also that they aren't that good at noticing when other people's experience is not the same as theirs. The second friend is showing you that they think of themselves as something of a victim and have chosen to focus on those parts of a situation that they see as unfair or unjust. The third friend seems to enjoy being a rebel and different from the rest of the group.

Instead of being amused or insulted by the rollercoaster surprise, he's curious and seems to want to return to master the situation.

Kinds of Meta-Programs

People are complicated. Though there may be predictable patterns, **most of us are complex and usually show a blend of different meta-programs**. The program can adapt depending on context, stress levels, and stage of life.

Nevertheless, the more we understand how other people make sense of their world, the more we understand them. This means we can communicate with them more easily, work with them, and speak their language in such a way as to get around any potential conflict or misunderstanding. Whether you want to create better rapport or simply adapt and adjust so you work around people, this NLP theory can help.

A meta-program is not exactly the same as a personality type, but it's close! That's because the mental program someone is running is precisely what allows them to form their own beliefs, perspectives, and opinions, and decides how they will organize meaning around their actions, their circumstances, and other people they encounter.

Here's an important thing to note: A meta-program is never "good" or "bad." It's neutral. It answers the question of what a person is going to focus on and what they filter out of awareness—none of us is omniscient, and simply by being alive, we apply mental filters to the world (you included). You could say that a person's way of doing this is unique to them and a prime determiner of their character. The only judgment we can apply here is whether this frame of reference is helping or hindering the person from achieving their stated aims (and again, their aims will be determined by their values, not necessarily yours).

Let's look at five common meta-programs used by NLP practitioners (there are seven, but we'll only consider the most common ones here) so we can better understand how to identify and work with each.

NLP Meta Program 1—Toward or Away

This is a question of "pain or gain." Does the person move *toward* something positive or *away* from something negative?

Tony Robbins, a popular NLP proponent, says,

> *"All human behavior revolves around the urge to gain pleasure or avoid pain. You pull away from a lighted match in order to avoid the pain of burning your hand. You sit and watch a beautiful sunset because you get pleasure from the glorious celestial show as day glides into night."*

"Toward" people are goal-oriented. They prioritize well and know what they want in life, as well as how to put that want front and center. They are motivated to always move toward something out there, in the future. Possibilities are imagined to be positive—however, there is sometimes so much positivity that critical thinking can take a back seat.

"Away" people are also motivated, but to get away from something. They're not crystal-clear on what they want, but they know very well what they *don't* want! Their focus on problems and potential obstacles makes them a bit of a stick in the mud, but on the other hand, they are more likely to anticipate snags and think more clearly and pragmatically about the future.

How can you tell the difference between them? Listen closely when people get very passionate about something. Are they excitedly talking about what they want and are striving for? Or are they passionately positioning themselves *against* something else? Let's say a person wants to lose weight. Notice how they talk about this goal. Is it "I'm going to look so hot when I reach my goal weight," or is it "If I don't turn my bad habits around, I'm going to kill myself"?

The difference can be subtle. Someone might *say* they're goal-oriented, but listen closely to how those goals are worded. "I want to not be fat anymore" is an *away* goal, whereas "I want to be thin" is a *toward* goal.

To connect with a toward person, you need to get on their wavelength and talk in such a way that centers their goal. If you're trying to convince them of something, focus on the long-term benefits and positive outcomes of what you're talking about, use expansive, inclusive body language, and look upward as though toward a bright future. To smooth over conflict with them, talk about the future and how things will be better then, and downplay what's already happened.

To connect with an away person, you need to frankly acknowledge the problem and, if you wish to motivate them, even hold them responsible for fixing it. If there's conflict, focus on what you're going to do to escape that conflict, rather than trying to smile and minimize—this might actually inspire them to dig their heels in!

Remember that no program is better than another—it's just a question of perspective. To talk to an away person, elaborate on the kind of situation you want to avoid, on risk, and on body language gestures that suggest exclusion. The key with this type of person is to mobilize their focus on the problem. Don't let them get diverted by crises, but ask what can be done to fix things.

Imagine that you yourself are primarily a toward person but you're talking to an away person. Because you understand this, you don't get frustrated with them being a stick in the mud about an exciting holiday you're planning together. When they keep homing in on potential disasters while you'd like to enjoy picturing how much fun you'll have, you decide that you won't argue with them or say things like "Don't be so negative! It'll never happen." Instead, you say, "Hm, maybe you're right about getting better travel insurance. Not having good coverage could be a nightmare. Could you shop around and find the best option for us?"

NLP Meta Program 2—External or Internal Frame of Reference

This "sort" basically depends on whether a person bases their standards on themselves or on others.

Internal frame-of-reference people are perceptive and self-centered. Here, the term isn't meant as an insult, but rather to show that such a person makes choices based on their own emotions and ideas. They process the world from the inside out. They must feel *personally* satisfied with their work or choice or they don't consider it valuable. Frequently, they give preference to their own intuitions and gut feeling over what others say they should think.

On the other hand, external frame-of-reference people concentrate on others and the value they imbue into things. They value other people's opinions because, for them, agreement, harmony, and consensus are precisely what give choices their value. This is the kind of person who is largely unclear about their thoughts, beliefs, and behaviors until they know what other people's are. They can easily imagine making a choice that is favored by the group whilst not necessarily valuing it themselves.

Robbins claims,

> "Ask someone else how he knows when he's done a good job. For some people, the proof comes from the outside. The boss pats you on the back and says your work is great. You get a raise. You win a big award. Your work is noticed and applauded by your peers.
>
> When you get that sort of external approval, you know your work is good. That's an external frame of reference. For others, the proof comes from inside. They

'just know inside' when they've done well."

To tell who you are dealing with, simply ask someone what their opinion is on a slightly contentious topic. You are listening not for what their answer is, but how they arrive at and justify that answer. Do they say "Well, I was raised Catholic, and we were taught X," or do they say "You'd be an idiot not to believe X"? Both these answers suggest they may be external. If they say "Well, a lot of people have different ideas" or "My personal feeling is X," then they may be more internal. While the body language for an internal type will be tight, closed, and focused on the self, the external type will be broader, more open, and less focused on the person.

Importantly, people can be internal or external while varying considerably in how much they actually conform to society's expectations, so don't let that fool you. For example, a person may do what their family/work/culture tells them, but resent the fact and see their actions as valueless. On the other hand, someone might appear to be a rebel or a black sheep, but deep down really crave societal approval—they're just bad at getting it! So, don't look at actions alone, but at the way people express themselves. Their choices matter, but *how they explain and justify those choices* matters more.

To connect with the internal type, the way is clear: Bear in mind that their source of value and meaning is internal. That means you speak about their experiences, wants, desires, needs, opinions, and so on. Frame the picture with them in the center, and there will seldom be any conflict. You make it so that they are deciding for themselves independently. These people have their own internally driven criteria—understand what they are and speak to them by framing your speech in terms of "I" and "you" and saying things like "personally . . ." or "that's your choice."

To connect with the external type, you must do the opposite: Introduce your own ideas or discuss others' ideas and how they might be useful. You are painting a harmonious picture and suggesting how they ought to fit into that. For example, you might invoke ideas such as duty or obligation, convention, law, tradition, authority, or even just fashion.

Think about a teacher who is trying to support the learning of two very different students. The first one he knows is an internal type, so when he gives feedback, he frames the student's performance in individualistic terms and refers to goals the student has set and to *their* values and principles. Where something is a problem, the teacher frames this problem as a violation of the student's own ethical code (even if the teacher doesn't agree with this code in the least).

However, in talking to another student who he knows is more external, he refers to their performance in relation to others in the class, to the teacher's own expectations or disappointments, and to the commonly held grade standards that determine that student's accomplishment. In dealing with more serious problems, the teacher might even mention the fact that the student's parents have paid a lot of money for school fees and will be upset that their child is not performing.

NLP Meta Program 3—Options or Procedures

Does the person enjoy choosing from many options or do they want to follow the set path already determined by the rules? In other words, what degree of autonomy does this person prefer?

The options type will actively seek out novelty and will value thinking outside the box. They want to be spontaneous and improvise.

The procedures type is not that thrilled with this approach and prefers to just use a tried-and-true method that has already been established. They value efficiency and productivity above being creative.

To connect with an options person, you need to... give them more options! Keep questions open-ended so you are always inspiring them to think about how they would create their own procedure. If you can, try to throw something unexpected into the mix—these people can be good problem-solvers if you gently direct their enthusiasm to all the possibilities around a current problem. Lean into their desire to sink their teeth into a complex problem.

For the procedure person, your focus in communication with them will always be on the HOW and not the WHY. They don't necessarily want to reinvent the wheel for every project; simply give them clear instructions that will help them get the task done as quickly as possible. Don't bother trying to convey the broader implications or get them enthusiastic—their lack of enthusiasm does *not* mean they won't work hard or well.

To tell the difference between an options person and a procedure person, pay attention to how they react to being given any type of task. Do they immediately start "playing" and trying to invent something new and different? Do they start trying to make something new or "explore the space"? They're an options thinker ("What can I do?").

Do they diligently get on with it and produce an efficient (if conventional) result? Do they ask what is ordinarily done and what has been done before? They're a procedures person ("What do I do?").

Imagine you're planning Christmas with family. Some of your family members are options people, so you know that when you talk with them about what they'll contribute to festivities, you inspire them by asking for fresh ideas or something new and different they can create ("Maybe we could do something totally different with the tree this year? Why don't you come up with something unconventional?").

With procedures people, you do none of this; you choose the quickest, most straightforward thing, then give them clear instructions for how to achieve that ("So you're in charge of Christmas Eve dinner, which is traditionally fish pie. I'll send you a recipe.") You probably can see that procedures people are often external, too.

NLP Meta Program 4—Matcher or Mismatcher

This key difference is about whether you focus on differences in relationships (mismatcher) or similarities (matcher).

Matchers are optimistic and approving and look for *commonalities* in conversations. They're all about harmony and cohesion. Thus, they base their decisions on similarities in others, circumstances, and life in general. They are always looking for the common denominator and value harmony and cooperation—which they may seek even to a fault.

The mismatchers take a different strategy and often prefer to rebel. Their tendency to be oppositional can sometimes manifest as creativity, quirkiness, or insightful critical reasoning, but just as often it comes out as fault-finding and general disagreeableness.

This is the kind of person who will automatically argue with you in a heated conversation . . . even if they don't actually have a strong opinion either way.

Tony Robbins believes there are two subtypes of mismatchers:

> "One type looks at the world and sees how things are different . . . The other kind of mis-matcher sees differences with exceptions."

Here, it's a question of what is seen first: Some people start with all the ways things are different, and then they build on to that the similarities. Others start with what is common and then look for exceptions.

In both cases, the way to determine which type someone may be is to pay attention to how they classify and perceive objects. For example, a matcher might look at a series of different-sized circles and notice one pertinent fact about them: "They're all circles." A mismatcher, however, will focus mainly on what is different: "They're all different sizes." Listen carefully if a person uses a lot of words that suggest difference:

but, although, however. They may also be away people, constantly defining themselves and their needs in opposition: "I'm *not* a conservative, I *don't* agree, I *can't* imagine that..."

With a little practice, you can hear this difference of orientation in the way people speak. Try to notice if their attention is always on what is the same or what is different. Are they always zooming in on the one tiny thing you two don't agree on? Or are they quite quick to round everybody up into the same category and look for common ground—even if there may be very little?

To connect with the matching type, lean into their tendency to find connections, and let them do the work—it's easy to find rapport with such a person since they will default to seeing you as similar to themselves. You can amplify that by mirroring—use similar language, spoken metaphors, gestures, etc. to cement your harmony. ("What are we going to do about this?"—the use of *we* comfortably implies similarity and cooperation.)

If you try to do this with a mismatcher, though, you will actually inspire the opposite reaction in them. That's what they're all about—opposites! Like many parents of rebellious teenagers know, you can go a long way with a little reverse psychology. If it's a given that they'll push against and disagree with whatever you propose, then propose the opposite of what you want them to do or see. ("Now, I'm pretty sure you're going to shoot this idea down, but what about if we . . .?" Here, you are working with the mismatcher's tendency to immediately respond, "You're actually wrong on that. I wouldn't shoot it down. In fact, I think it's a great idea.")

NLP Meta Program 5—Necessity or Possibility

Finally, notice whether someone makes decisions based on maximizing or simply satisfying. According to Robbins,

> "[Necessity people] are not pulled to take action by what is possible. They're not looking for infinite varieties of experience.
>
> They go through life taking what comes and what is available. When they need a new job or a new house or a new car or even a new spouse,

> they go out and accept what is available.
>
> Others are motivated to look for possibilities. They're motivated less by what they have to do than by what they want to do. They seek options, experiences, choices, paths."

For those more focused on necessity, there is a lot of value in "settling." They are happy to avoid the bad thing, and don't necessarily value looking around for alternatives and variety. For them, comfort and consolidation provide a lot of satisfaction. The irony is that such a person is more likely to be satisfied with life and better positioned to maximize on the opportunities that are actually in their world, instead of entertaining a bunch of pie-in-the-sky dreams. However, they may just as easily fail to peak out of their comfort zones, with underwhelming results.

For those more focused on possibility, there is a lot of excitement to be had in variety and opportunities for things to be different. They would prefer to pursue something enticing and unknown than to settle for the default. They take chances. These carry risks and costs, *sometimes enormous ones*, but also occasionally result in growth, which they highly prize.

To connect with a necessity person, remember that it's useless to focus on "what if"—this is not exciting for such a person. It may even be intimidating or unsettling. Instead, look at what actually *already is* and focus on the positives that are there. The idea is to amplify feelings of familiarity, security, ease, and safety. Find reasons for why the choice already made was a good one, rather than asking what choices could be made in the future.

A possibility person has a completely different motivation, so when you are attempting to communicate with them, you need to more heavily favor what could be rather than what is. In a way, the split between necessity and possibility is the divide between conservative and progressive (in the psychological, not the political sense). Because possibility is about growth, development, exploration, and novelty, you would do well to frame any course of action in terms of its potential. Focusing on the benefits of staying the same (i.e., conserving) will leave possibility people uninspired and unconvinced. Alternatively, focus on the idea of challenge and encourage them to weigh up risk and reward and to chart a course into the future.

How can you tell which one a person is? Ask them some kind of "why" question. For example, "Why did you take this current job?" or "Why did you choose to live in this neighborhood?" Then listen to the kind of answer you're given (important—not the content of the answer, but the way this content is framed). If they frequently use language along the lines of "need" and "have to," then they are operating from necessity—"We had to be near the school" or "I needed the money!" If they answer with language more to do with "want," then they are more likely running the possibility meta-program—"We wanted to be closer to nature" or "I wanted to challenge myself in a new role." Listen for other meta-programs—this one overlaps predictably with the away and toward meta-program.

Now, knowing all this about each of the meta-programs, it's worth bearing in mind that it takes some skill to identify these models in others. Not least because you have a meta-program, too, and will be seeing them through *your* filter!

Always remember that meta-programs depend on context, are stress-related, and may change over time. So, don't notice one event and assume you know everything about the person. Instead, notice stable and recurring patterns. Another thing to be cognizant of is what your intentions are. If you are merely seeking to understand another person, then do so by **working with their meta-program**, not opposing it. If you are trying to communicate well and establish rapport, then it is not your job to challenge, diagnose, or convince. Understanding your own meta-program will help you make changes, but unless you're a therapist or a motivational speaker, there's seldom a need to enter social interactions with the agenda of changing people's fundamental perspectives.

Finally, keep in mind that **this theory is also best understood contextually and relatively.** People do not exist in a vacuum, and their mental models are not static. Notice how they are interacting with their environment and with other people, and how their meta-programs are actually functioning. In other words, if you want to quickly understand how someone ticks, ask what function their mental model is actually serving. **They think that way for a reason. What's the reason?** Look at the way they respond to other people, to challenges, to opportunities, to ambiguity, etc. This will tell you a lot about the invisible mental programming they're running.

Summary:

- Meta programs are our mental maps or representations of reality. To better read people, fully understand we need only pay attention to their words, body language, and actions and infer the meta-programs they are running. Most people show a blend of different programs and can change over time.
- Identify the meta-program and then work with it to create harmony and understanding, remembering that meta-programs are contextual, relative, and influenced by stress.
- One program is whether they move *toward* something positive or *away* from something negative. Observe what people are passionate about and how they frame their motivations.
- Another program is *external* versus *Internal* frame of reference—i.e., whether a person bases their standards on themselves or on others.

To test this, ask questions about the person's source of value or satisfaction, or ask their opinion on a slightly contentious topic, and observe how they justify and explain their choice.
- Discern between *options* versus *procedure* thinking—i.e., the degree of novelty, autonomy, and spontaneity a person prefers. To tell the difference, pay attention to how a person reacts to being given a task.
- Discern between *matchers* and *mismatchers*—i.e., whether someone focuses on similarities or differences. Observe the way they classify and group objects—according to similarity or difference?
- Finally, discern between *necessity* or *possibility* mindsets—i.e., maximizing or simply satisfying. Ask a "why" question and listen for "need to" versus "have to" clues.

Chapter 9: Keep Your Ears Pricked for Word Clues

If you want to know who people are, simply listen—they will *tell* you!

No, they will seldom spell it out directly, but if you know how to "listen between the lines," there is a whole world of insight you can glean from a person's ordinary speech.

Some particular word choices reveal things about the person who chose them. John Schafer, an FBI behavior analyst, called these especially revealing words Word Clues. By looking at the words people use when they talk or write, Word Clues help you understand what motivates people, predict how they will behave, and get a deeper understanding of how they see their world.

Of course, Word Clues can't tell you *everything* about a person's personality, but they can give you a starting point. Word Clues are a great way to come up with an initial hypothesis about someone. With more in-depth observations, you can then test this hypothesis and gradually confirm your original hunches. All you have to do is listen carefully, identify certain words, and then make educated guesses about what these word choices suggest.

A key part of Schafer's theory is that **when people think, they do so using only verbs and nouns. Other parts of speech—adjectives and adverbs, especially—are added on purpose after the fact. *Why* they are added reveals something about the speaker** and what they are trying to achieve and why. If you simply notice adjectives and adverbs in everyday speech, you will more readily notice this form of bias that people can't help but reveal. As an example everyone will understand immediately, imagine someone tells you, "A black man killed that beautiful young woman." You'd instantly wonder *why* the adjectives "black," "young," and "beautiful" were included.

For a more subtle example, imagine someone is telling you an anecdote, and they say at some point, "I walked quickly." You notice this word "quickly" and how it's not really an integral part of the meaning of the story. The person is telling a story about something else entirely, but they add in this tiny detail about how quickly they walked to get to the train and arrive at a meeting. "Quickly" becomes a Word Clue for you. It gives a sense of urgency, but it doesn't explain *why* the urgency is there. But you can guess: You might walk quickly because you're afraid of being late to a meeting you're going to and of the disappointment of breaking a social norm or expectation.

Perhaps, given the context and what you know of this person, it might suggest that they wish to be thought of as reliable and trustworthy. They want to live up to expectations. Or, another interpretation still is that the word implies a more general sense of anxiety and heightened tension. "Quickly" can suggest haste, even a tiny bit of fear. Either way, the fact that the person has included it in a story that isn't actually about their being on time at all tells you something.

What does it tell you? Well, the rest of the conversation will help you decide. But what's important is that your observation is a *clue*— not a full-blown conclusion about anything, just a clue. A hint. A suggestion. If you find several other such hints and suggestions in the person's speech, you gradually get to confirm one of your original hypotheses. For example, if the person uses lots of other adverbs to suggest promptness, correctness, and reliability, even when these details are not crucial to the story at hand, then you can be sure that you are dealing with someone who is conscientious, eager to please, and observant of social etiquette.

The next time you're talking with someone, tune out the content for a moment and listen to the word choice they are making.

1. Identify the core, necessary parts of speech—verbs and nouns
2. Identify everything else
3. Then ask what this "everything else" means—why was it chosen and not something else?

For a very basic example, imagine that your aunt arrives at your house unannounced one day. She says to you, "Oh, I'm sorry. I was in the neighborhood, so I thought I'd just come over for a teeny tiny visit. Hopefully you still like almond cookies, right?"

The core of this piece of communication is: "I came to visit."

Everything else is extra:

The fact that she is sorry (i.e., aware that you won't like her coming unannounced).

The fact that she feels it necessary to justify her visit (being in the neighborhood).

She *just* came over for a *teeny tiny* visit (this adverb and adjective combination suggests she doesn't want to intrude, but downplays the inconvenience she might be causing).

She has brought cookies expressly for you (the "hopefully" suggesting that they are a kind of offering to offset showing up unannounced, and the "still" carrying all sorts of connotations—it implies that she has known you for a long time, that she is familiar with your tastes, but that she won't assume they have stayed the same, etc.).

Can you see how the bulk of what your aunt is really saying is *outside* of the main components of the message itself? All you need to do to confirm this is to change these extra details while still keeping the central message intact, noticing how much it changes everything:

"I've brought you some almond cookies. Well, are you going to invite me in? Or is the place a mess?"

Or what about:

"Hello, hello, hello! It's your favorite aunt! Surprise! You are going to just die when you see what I've brought for you."

Of course, you'd be exhausted if you had to analyze every sentence out of every person's mouth, but it is good to remember that nothing that people say or do is ever really neutral. Remind yourself that people are often in the position of being able to say absolutely anything at all, but they choose one specific thing. *Why?* Answering that question gives you a glimpse into their world.

Let's look at a few more examples.

"I won another award."

The Word Clue "another" not only makes the point that the speaker won previous awards, but also that they wish to draw your attention to this fact. This person wanted to ensure that other people know that he or she won at least one other award, thus bolstering his or her self-image. If you notice other corroborating Word Clues of this kind, you can safely conclude that this person needs or enjoys the adulation of others to reinforce their self-esteem.

Observers could exploit this vulnerability by using flattery and other ego-enhancing comments; alternatively, you can connect more deeply with such a person knowing that their self-worth is a tender point and a potential inroad to more authenticity in future communication with them.

"I worked hard to achieve my goal."

All achievements require work. But if someone emphasizes the *hardness* of the work, what does it imply? The Word Clue "hard" may suggest this person values goals that are difficult to achieve, precisely because of their difficulty. They may relish a challenge, seeing its difficulty as proof of the value of any action.

But you could read other things in this word, too. Someone who not just works, but works hard, wants to emphasize not just the fact of their having competed a task, but of how much they deserve that outcome. This Word Clue can suggest pride or even a sense of entitlement or defensiveness. You can almost imagine it following the unspoken sentence "I know others get things in life for free, but . . . I worked *hard* for it."

Finally, listen for other Word Clues, since other interpretations are possible. For example, someone may say this a few times specifically to emphasize that it was not luck or talent that won, but sheer grunt work. They may have a strong desire to be recognized for their work, or even for others to admire them or acknowledge the sacrifices they made. Compare the following two pairs of statements and notice how, in context, the Word Clue "hard" suggests different interpretations.

"Growing up, I had none of the support you kids have today. I worked hard to achieve my goal."

"I know some people find a bachelor's degree a walk in the park, but I don't care. I worked hard to achieve my goal."

See the difference context makes?

"I patiently sat through the lecture."

Another adverb that tells a story.

The Word Clue "patiently" presents several hypotheses. Perhaps this person is bored with the lecture. Maybe they don't think very highly of the lecturer, or maybe they think very highly of their own mastery of the subject. Regardless of the reason, this person is preoccupied with something other than the content of the lecture ... and yet chose to stay in the lecture. Furthermore, they want to *tell* you about this discrepancy. Note, they don't say "I went to the lecture." They are communicating something additional with the Word Clue "patiently." What could it be?

Perhaps this is a person who adheres to social norms and etiquette but doesn't especially like doing so and wants you to know that while they'll follow certain rules, that doesn't mean they like them! After all, a person who doesn't care about social rules will just leave a lecture if they're not enjoying it. They will not present this action as something out of the ordinary, either.

So what does it mean if a person does frame a situation this way? Let's say you form the hypothesis: "this person is externally motivated. They're fair and law abiding, but a little passive." Later, you notice again that they complain a few times about things they're uncomfortable with, but you also notice they make no efforts to improve the situation or get away from it in any way. This kind of thing is subtle but powerful—you are noticing that this person has a very external locus of control.

So what? Well, people with external loci of control are those who tend not to take responsibility for their own lives, but who see occurrences, good or bad, as always stemming from other people or circumstances, and not their own volition. This is a pretty good thing to know when it comes to choosing a running partner to keep you accountable to your fitness commitments, right? You can predict that this is the kind of person who will avoid a workout and then blame something or someone else.

"I decided to buy that model."

On the other hand, here is a person who is telling you, with this Word Clue "decided," that they are the autonomous, active agents in their lives and that things are happening because they *choose* for them to happen. While someone could simply tell you what they bought, here is a person who wants to emphasize the fact that this outcome was deliberately created by themselves. Why?

The word indicates that this person weighed various options prior to the purchase. Perhaps they struggled to some degree before deciding. They may want to communicate that this was not some haphazard thing, but a process of careful deliberation. Combined with other clues, this might suggest you are talking to someone who is not impulsive. Unlike, for example, the person who says "I just bought this model." "Just" strongly communicates impulsivity, indifference, or spontaneity. The action is not something they value or focus on.

"I did the right thing."

The Word Clue "right" suggests that this person struggled with a legal, moral, or ethical dilemma and overcame some level of internal or external opposition to make a fair and just decision. You are speaking to someone with a pronounced sense of right and wrong. They frame their actions in terms of some objective measure of truth. Compare this, for example, with someone who says, "I did the best thing for me," or even, "I did what I was supposed to." The meaning could not be more different, right?

A person who litters their speech with reference to goodness and rightness is, obviously, sending a message not just that they hold personal values, but that they believe in some higher, objective ethical standards, and more than that, they wish to align themselves with that. In other words, you're dealing with a pretty trustworthy and scrupulous person!

"It was done..."

Listen for people who frequently use passive voice when they speak, rather than active voice. To quickly explain:

The dog bit Johnny (active).

Johnny was bitten (passive).

The way that people order the subject and the object in a sentence tells you a lot about how they view culpability, agency, and choice. You can immediately see in the example above that the first sentence centers the dog and very clearly identifies it as the agent who did an action—biting. The second sentence, however, puts Johnny in the center, and the dog becomes less important, or even invisible. What matters more is that someone was bitten, and not *who* did the biting.

With this in mind, it's easy to read certain implications in someone's claim "I'm sorry you were hurt," when they could have just as easily said "I'm sorry I hurt you." If people suddenly switch to passive voice, ask why. Are they trying to downplay someone's agency—likely their own? They may be running an external reference meta-program and don't truly see themselves as responsible or to blame. This distinction goes beyond just the grammatical fact of passive voice, though. For example, compare the difference between "we arrived at the party" and "I took us to the party." The latter is more concerned with the agency and actions of one specific person than the action itself. If a person is repeatedly talking about themselves this way, you can infer that they see themselves in the driver's seat (in this case, literally!) and that this is the most salient feature of this situation for them.

A final word of warning here: While FBI agents and interrogators have to come to life-or-death conclusions based on very little information, you can give yourself a bit more leeway. No single Word Clue is enough on its own. Rather, look for **recurring patterns of words** and ask what broader meaning these choices convey about the person who chose them and not some other words.

Listening to Tone of Voice

As the old saying goes, it's not what you do, it's the way that you do it. Or to put it another way, it's not what you say, it's the way that you say it.

A person's tone of voice may be one of the most meaningful components of what they're communicating to you. Consciously or unconsciously, people convey enormous amounts of information in the timbre, speed, clarity, tone, volume and projection of their voice—no matter what particular words they are or aren't saying!

If a dozen people all say the same sentence, they'll each do it completely uniquely, and their different tones of voice will tell you a lot about their different psychological states (not to mention the facts that their accents and voice "age" will tell you loads, too—but that's for another chapter).

The Laboratory of Instrumental Analysis of Communication at the Autonomous University of Barcelona conducted a research study investigating tone of voice and perception. Their findings were fascinating. They discovered that deeper voices were associated with maturity, while higher tones were perceived to carry less credibility. However, extremely deep ones could go too far and convey something more sinister. Talking very quietly was perceived as weak or unconfident.

The big question here is, if we perceive these things to be true, does that mean they're *actually* true? While there probably are socialized and arbitrary elements (for example, it wouldn't be fair to say that women, who have naturally higher-pitched voices, are all uniformly less credible than men, who have naturally lower voices), we can nevertheless make some educated guesses about the variations in voice that are *not* genetic and unchangeable.

Breath

When you think about it, the voice is made out of breath. How someone speaks comes down to their mastery and regulation of air flow from the lungs over the vocal cords. If someone's voice is calm and even, then it's likely they feel calm and even, too. A person who speaks as though they're constantly running out of air is telling you that they are nervous, unsure, or rushed.

Volume

How loud we speak conveys plenty of information about how much "aural space" we are comfortable taking up. People who talk loudly or even over others (or screaming babies, for that matter) are conveying that they feel confident and even entitled to dominate the airwaves in such a way.

A person talking quietly, though, isn't always telling you that they're timid. In certain contexts, speaking quietly can convey an extremely strong and self-assured sense of confidence, or else can even be seductive; when someone whispers, they may be deliberately drawing us in closer to them so we can hear—it's a power move.

Articulation

Think of vocal expression in terms of agility. Is the person talking with clarity, ease, and control, moving with precision and proficiency? Or is their speech chaotic, imprecise, stumbling, inelegant, or filled with "ums" and "likes"? Vocal mastery is almost always a reflection of some other form of mastery. They may be intelligent, knowledgeable, experienced, well organized, or on the ball in some other way (or, at the very least, they *think* of themselves in this way!).

Speed

Speed of speech tells you a lot about emotional state and degree of excitement. If the speed is slow and ponderous, there's a lack of interest there, or even a disconnect (it's important to see the source of this indifference, though—is it the topic being discussed, the audience, or life in general? Do they just not like *you*?). A rapid speed can suggest excitement, but also tension or a feeling of being rushed. An irregular speed suggests confusion on the part of the speaker, or that communication breakdown is occurring.

Pitch

Research by the University of Göttingen published in the *Journal of Research in Personality* suggests that a lower-pitched voice is associated with people who are more dominant, extroverted, or higher in "sociosexuality" (which means more interested in casual sex or sex outside a relationship). They claimed these findings were true for both men and women.

The researchers asked two thousand people to complete personality tests, and then analyzed recordings of their voices so that pitch could be measured objectively by computers.

According to research lead Dr. Julia Stern,

> "Even if we just hear someone's voice without any visual clues—for instance, on the phone—we know pretty soon whether we're talking to a man, a woman, a child, or an older person. We can pick up on whether the person sounds interested, friendly, sad, nervous, or whether they have an attractive voice. We also start to make assumptions about trust and dominance."

Stern's research shows that we may be right to make these assumptions after all!

An easy tip to learning to read people's tone of voice is to simply become more aware of your own. After all, you always know how you feel in situations; pay attention to how this manifests in your voice. What is true for you is probably true for others.

A fun exercise to try is to watch movies, but in a language foreign to you. Listen closely to how the actors and actresses are speaking, and try to glean as much information from this as possible. If you like, to train yourself to focus on the sound alone, you could even close your eyes and completely remove the visual element. What can you guess about the way they are feeling just from the quality of their voice?

Understand Function Words

Can pronoun use tell you anything about a person? According to James Pennebaker's research in the 90s, yes. He helped develop software that analyzed various texts, including student essays, IMs, press conference transcripts, and more. This research revealed that "function words" (words like pronouns, articles, prepositions, conjunctions, and auxiliary verbs) give more important clues to a person's emotional state than do "content words" (i.e., the ordinary nouns, adverbs, verbs, etc.).

According to Pennebaker,

"Function words help shape and shortcut language. People require social skills to use and understand function words, and they're processed in the brain differently. They are the key to understanding relationships between speakers, objects, and other people. When we analyze people's use of function words, we can get a sense of their emotional state and personality, and their age and social class."

Pronouns tell us where we have put our focus. Imagine you ask someone what the weather is. Consider these two possible answers:

1. It's hot.
2. I think it's hot.

That little extra pronoun in the second option seems small, but it makes a big difference. It shows a focus on the self. If you had a hunch that the person you were talking to had an internal frame of reference, this would certainly be a clue to support that hypothesis. Interestingly, Pennebaker found that depressed people use "I" more often than non-depressed people. Now that's something to listen out for!

Pennebaker also believes that people who are lying tend to use "we" more often or avoid first-person pronouns, almost as an unconscious bid to rope you in on the reality they're trying to sell you. Those intending to deceive or obscure their culpability will often make generalized statements that include everyone else. For example, they won't say, "I didn't take the money" but something like, "These days, everyone knows you can't just leave money lying around like that." On the other hand, repeated use of "we" in certain contexts could indicate a strong social bond—or the desire for or assumption of one.

People who heavily use articles (like "a," "an," and "the") are communicating a concrete style of thinking, i.e., they tend to see ideas, situations, and even people as things or objects in their field. Conversely, people who tend to refer to things and situations in relational terms are telling you that they predominantly focus on relationships and dynamics between people. Compare, for example, the difference between saying "I'll bring my wife" versus "I'll bring the wife."

It's important to state here that these findings were made using computer software to analyze very small differences in speech—in other words, variations that were too tiny to be perceived in ordinary interactions. In addition, they applied to populations, not individuals. That doesn't mean you can't use their insights in your own life to better read people; it just means that you will need to clock many more **repeated instances** of a particular language clue before you can conclude anything meaningful.

How Language Reflects a Person's Meta-Program

You've probably noticed that there is significant overlap in how we interpret Word Clues, tone of voice, and function words, and how we analyze the meta-program a person is running. Let's say you're trying to determine if a person is using the NLP meta-program of internal or external reference. You listen closely and the person drops Word Clues:

"I chose to do XYZ because . . ."
"I decided to . . ."
"I married him . . ."

You notice that the person has a tendency to choose words that reflect their own agency, volition, and choice. Totally an internal reference! What's more, you suspect they may be more oriented toward options than they are to procedures because they tend to focus on the available possibilities and what they personally wish to do with those options. You notice loads of "I" statements (for example, this person doesn't say "we got married" or "he married me," but "*I* married *him*"), showing you that they have an internal, individual focus.

Imagine now that all of this is delivered in a tone of voice that is quiet, high pitched, and rapid. Sentences are long and complex but rushed, without you being able to get a word in. Are you beginning to get a richer sense of who this person is? You might hypothesize that this person is dominant, a little self-absorbed, and highly energetic, but that at their core, they are slightly insecure and in a hurry to prove something.

Luckily for you, you can build on this hypothesis with every conversation, and with focused listening and careful inference-making, you can begin to see deeply inside this person's head and at things they themselves might not even be aware of! But you don't have to do all this guesswork in the dark. There is one very obvious way to directly test and refine your hypotheses, and that's to ask questions.

Summary:

- People think in verbs and nouns with other parts of speech added after the fact. These additional word choices reveal a lot about a person and can be considered Word Clues. Pay attention to adverb use and the story they tell about how the person sees themselves and others. Notice what is emphasized and what is ignored, and especially pay attention to recurring patterns of words.
- Tone of voice is a part of body language and may be one of the most meaningful components of what a person is communicating. Notice breath (fast and shallow suggest excitement or anxiety), volume (loud suggests confidence or aggression), articulation (correlates with clarity and organization of thought), speed, and pitch.
- "Function words" (such as pronouns, articles, prepositions, conjunctions, and auxiliary verbs) give more important clues to a person's mindset

than do "content words." They tell you about the way the speaker understands relationships, objects, and the world in general, as well as all about their emotional state, personality, age, and social class. High personal pronoun use suggests a focus on the self, liars tend to focus on "we," and heavy article use (a, the) suggests a concrete thinking style.
- There is significant overlap in Word Clues, tone of voice and function words, and the meta-program a person is running. Listen carefully for words that signal things like internal or external frame of reference, necessity of possibility thinking, or matching versus mismatching focus.

Chapter 10: The Art of Asking the Right Questions

You can tell a lot about somebody by reading their body language and looking at their clothing, their posture, their accent, the words they use, the things they *don't* say, and their facial expressions. But at some point, you're going to need to go a little deeper and get more detailed information. And sometimes, the only way to get that information is to come out and ask. However, **there are a million ways to ask a question, and sometimes the best ones are those that get us the information we want while appearing on the surface to be completely unrelated.**

Let's take a closer look at how to ask questions that really help you learn the most you can about people.

The Kipling Method

In general, the 5W1H is a way to ask questions and solve problems and is meant to help you see ideas and problems from different points of view. It helps you get to the bottom of a problem and figure out how to fix it. It's pretty straightforward: the acronym stands for what, where, when, why, and who, with the letter H standing in for how.

5W1H is also called the Kipling method after the British author and poet Rudyard Kipling, who came up with it. Kipling used five W questions in his poem "The Elephant's Child," which is the story of an extremely curious elephant who is interested in everything around him. It may sound obvious, but in reading and analyzing people, we can use the Kipling method to help us structure our efforts to gather information that will help us understand a person better.

What

We often ask "What" to seek things that are and will be. We can use this when we are interested to know something specific about a person.

Examples:

- What do you intend to do?
- What do you enjoy doing?
- What pisses you off?

Why

When you ask "why," you are looking for links between causes and effects. This question word probes for a far more sophisticated depth of understanding. Knowing what someone has done doesn't always give you insight into their reasons and motivations. But if you know *why* people have done something, you can begin to understand the world of meaning they have constructed for themselves in their own heads.

Examples:

- Why did you do that?
- Why did that happen?
- Why is it important for us to try it again?

When

When looks for a place in time and can mean two different things—either a point in time that has passed or one that might still come. When can be used to ask for a single specific time, like when someone will arrive at a certain place or when something will be done.

Examples:

- When will you be finished?
- When should we meet?
- When did you give me the money?

How

How is a question that asks for "verbs of process." In other words, the answer is usually an adverb. Knowing what we know about how adverbs are almost always powerful Word Clues, we can ask how to dig deeper into what has happened or what will happen.

Examples:

- How did you do that?

- How did you get everybody's attention?
- How are you finding this project?

Where

Where tries to locate an action or event in three-dimensional space. This can be a simple space, such as on, above, under, or below, or something like a country, a building, a type of location, or even a vague context or environment. When a person answers this kind of question, they are giving you valuable information about how they contextualize and locate certain ideas.

Examples:

- Where did you get that bubbly personality?
- Where did you study?
- Where is this relationship going?

Who

Who brings people into the picture and links them to actions and things. It's a question that directly inquires about the relational human aspects to any situation. The most interesting people in any scenario tend to be the ones who are causing an action, or else deriving a benefit or penalty from that action.

Examples:

- Who is this work for?
- Who will benefit most from what you propose?
- Who else would be interested?

Though the above might seem pretty elementary, we can sometimes forget that **the questions we ask play a major role in the type of information we're likely to extract from someone.** Let's imagine that we're talking to the woman we introduced in the previous section—the one who says "I married him" rather than "he married me." Let's say that, given all your observations, you make a hypothesis about her motivation as a person: You guess that she is very goal-oriented and independent.

So you ask her some questions and notice that almost all of her answers begin with "I think" or "I feel." When you ask a *how* question, she answers with statements about how she achieved something, what she wanted, what she chose, and what she thought of the outcome. When you ask her a *why* question, you notice that she doesn't attribute many outcomes to random chance or the actions of others, but rather to her own actions. Incidentally, you also notice that she appears to quite enjoy being asked questions of this kind and is happy to talk about herself . . .

Bit by bit, your questions mine for data that you use to strengthen and refine the working model you have of her. All questions will yield interesting information, but *why* and *how* questions tend to be more open-ended and invite more colorful responses. These are the ones most likely to give you an insight into how a person thinks.

On the other hand, pay attention to the kind of questions the person is asking you. When you bear in mind that it's recurrent patterns that matter and never just a single question, it's obvious that a person's question shows you what they're most interested in.

Who? This is a person who is interested in relationships and people.
What? The details matter to them.
Where, when? They have a more procedural view and want to construct a narrative in a time and place.

Why? This person is interested in cause and effect, motivations, meaning, and bigger-picture ideas.

How? As above, but the person is asking for more explanation, detail, and nuance.

The questions a person chooses to ask can tell you what they see as the most important element of a situation. For example:

"I got a C minus in math again."
"What?! Who is your teacher?"

Assumptive Questions

Imagine there is an ad in a beauty magazine. The ad copy says *stop wasting money on harsh drying toners* and *we love simplicity as much as you do.*

The ad has made certain forceful assumptions—namely that you are the kind of person who not only knows what toner is, but uses it, spends a lot of money on it, and is dissatisfied with it, finding it dry and harsh. You are also assumed to be a lover of simplicity. The conclusion is that you are like the people writing the ad, and so ought to buy whatever they're selling.

While marketers use assumptions like this to artificially create the kind of consumer they want for their product and generate the sort of desire that results in profit, the same technique can be used to confirm your own hypotheses about people and to sneakily pose a statement as a question.

Consider these examples, which all *look* like questions, but aren't. In order to answer them, you have to accept the hidden assumption within:

- How much do you care? (Assumption: you do care)
- How will you persuade her? (Assumption: you want to persuade her and are going to do it, it's possible to persuade her in the first place, and perhaps there are many different ways to choose between).
- Where do you buy your cheese? (Assumption: you buy cheese!)
- What are you avoiding admitting to yourself? (Assumption: there is something you are avoiding, you know what it is, and the person asking the question is entitled to be told all about it).

Simply by framing a question a certain way, we are implying something about the possibilities for the form the answer will take. The way the other person chooses to respond to these implications can speak volumes. Let's imagine you ask the woman in our example, "So what do you think your biggest flaws are?" and you notice that she can't quite answer the question, or says something like, "I guess people can find my confidence a little intimidating . . ." This tells you that the hidden assumption (i.e., that she has flaws) is actually not something she acknowledges—that is not part of her own mental model. But if you had asked outright, "Are you a little arrogant?" you would not have received such a revealing answer!

On the other hand, the questions that people ask *you* can also reveal their own assumptions, biases, and preconceptions. If someone asks, "So, was his proposal really romantic?" they are not just assuming that there was a proposal, but conveying a whole world of value judgments and expectations. They are asking you about the thing that *they* are focused on and value. Even though they are asking the questions and you are answering, you are actually gleaning information about their values, priorities, and meta-programs! Consider this exchange and see what the question implies about the asker's values and frame of reference:

A: I've gone vegan. It's been six months now!
B: Oh my God, good on you! Tell me, how much weight have you lost? Do you find your skin is much clearer?

Chunking Up and Chunking Down

"Chunking" is the act of putting together or breaking up information or data into bigger or smaller pieces. In conversation, it's a way to ask questions or organize ideas in such a way as to reach an agreement or gain clarification. But the way that people use chunking in their own speech can tell you interesting things about them as people—if you pay attention!

"Chunking up" is when you move from specific and detailed information to more general or abstract information. How and why questions tend to lead to chunking up.
"Chunking down" goes the other way and happens whenever we move from broad generalizations and abstractions down to finer specifics. Where, what, when, and who questions tend to lead to chunking down.

When you chunk up, it is as though you are zooming out of the conversation to gain a broad, top-down overview of it, or as though you were getting a more general but larger "map" of the terrain of the conversation. When you chunk down, it's like taking a deep dive or getting stuck back into the nitty-gritty level, filling in the inevitable gaps you have on a more abstract overview.

Understanding how chunking works can help you in three ways:

1. It can help you structure your own questions so that you zoom in and out of the topic appropriately, helping you gain a detailed but also broad understanding of what the other person is trying to share with you.
2. It can help you understand how the other person is using chunking, and what this implies about how they're structuring their own mental maps.
3. It can help you identify differences in chunking styles—typically, misunderstandings and conflicts arise from a mismatch of chunking styles. Making sure that chunking styles are

balanced and aligned can smooth over conversational difficulties.

So how do you use chunking in a conversation where you're trying to learn more about a person?

First, chunking up questions will help you zoom out and find commonality, look for themes, or help you summarize what you've been told so you can reflect it, showing that you understand and are paying attention.

A: So after we lived in Puerto Rico for a while, we found ourselves back in Italy, but within just two months, because of work, we found ourselves pulling the kids out of school again and doing a year-long stint in France. We wanted to come back to Puerto Rico, but . . . oh well, long story short, we're here in New Zealand instead!

B: Wow, what a whirlwind! So overall you moved, what, four times in one year?!

A: Pretty much.

B: What toll do you think all that had on you?

A: Well, it was hard, but we all learned a lot, I will say that.

Speaker B above has asked two chunking up questions. The first more or less summarizes the key theme of the story ("a whirlwind!"), and the second probes a little for bigger overarching themes that connected all these disparate travel experiences. The question itself is looking for a broader, more abstract analysis, rather than any tiny details about what happened in each particular country, or the exact dates they went there.

If Speaker B continues asking these kinds of chunking up questions, eventually the pair might find themselves having a very detached and abstracted conversation, indeed, about how humankind has always been nomadic, the resilience of children, globalization, the philosophical and political implications of being dislocated from the land, etc.

If A and B are enjoying this, it *may* be a good conversation, but it probably won't be a conversation in which they learn much about one another as people!

Adding some chunking down questions will not only make for a more balanced and comfortable conversation, it will allow more personal and detailed information to come through. The devil is in the details, but so are people's more interesting idiosyncrasies. A good rule of thumb is to stick to no more than three questions of one type in a row. If you ask three chunking up questions, switch to a chunking down question to drill down a little more deeply into a specific idea or detail. But don't stay there too long or you'll risk getting "caught in the weeds." Come up for air after a few chunking down questions to get a breather and a bird's-eye view:

B: What toll do you think all that had on you?

A: Well, it was hard, but we all learned a lot, I will say that.

B: So be honest, which country was your favorite?

A: Hm ... honestly? I thought I'd love France, but it was nothing like I'd imagined. I'm really loving New Zealand, which I never expected to.

B: What surprised you most about France?

You can almost imagine zooming in on the mental map, from countries to favorite countries to France to something specific about France. But if Speaker A had said, "You know what, they all drink too much!" and Speaker B had another fifty questions about what kind of wine, the conversation would not only stall, but they'd stop gaining further insight into Speaker A.

Here are some examples of chunking-up-style questions (importantly, these are not necessarily verbatim):

What do you think that means?
Why did that happen?
So in the bigger picture...?
Is that connected to...?
What do you think that says about...?
How do all these things connect?
What do you think of...?
How do you make sense of...?

Here are some examples of chunking-down-style questions:

How did you like that?
What happened?
What happened next?

When ... ?
Who did that?
Tell me more about ...

So, if you make sure to balance the ratio of chunking up and chunking down questions in any conversation, you'll likely keep things moving along at an enjoyable and balanced pace. But pay attention to learn more about your conversation party.

Do they continually ask chunking up questions themselves and respond most enthusiastically to chunking up questions from you? This could mean a few things. Organizing, analytical, and pattern-seeking activity typically show intelligence, awareness, and mastery of a topic, but it can also hint at a desire to be personally and emotionally distant from a certain topic. If you're having a heated conversation with someone and they suddenly seem to retreat into lofty abstractions about nobody in particular, ask whether you've struck a nerve and if chunking up is serving as an evasive maneuver.

Do they continually ask chunking down questions or respond most enthusiastically to yours? This could indicate a narrow, focused, or even enthusiastic sense of attention to concrete matters, but it can also signal a lack of insight and critical thinking. People most comfortable continually chunking down could be read as running the procedural meta-program and may feel bored or lost in a conversation that doesn't anchor directly onto something in their literal lives in that moment. On the other hand, someone asking chunking down questions could be signaling that they are interested not in the topic at hand, but in *you*. You'll notice that people who flirt, for example, are seldom having a deep and meaningful conversation!

Finally, if you do notice that someone prefers chunking down, pay attention to the kind of questions they ask to gain insight into what they're primarily focused on. Are they more interested in people, places, what happened, the prices of things, family connections, the sequence of events? If you're talking very generally, notice what triggers people to dive deeper into detail. They are communicating what inspires and excites them. By the same token, someone who repeatedly chunks up while you're trying to chunk down might be telling you that they don't find that particular topic very interesting!

You may be wondering if every question is potentially a chunking up or chunking down question. The answer is yes! That said, there are also questions you could ask that act to keep the conversation at more or less the same level of depth—i.e., they neither chunk up or down but stay at that level of focus.

At the end of the day, it's not any particular question itself that will yield greater or lesser insight into someone's character. Rather, it's how that question is used. This is why it's important to create hypotheses in your mind to explain your perceptions and observations. That way, you "test" that observation through targeted questions. At the same time, you listen to their questions, what they are probing for, what they are focusing on, and what that tells you about their motivations, priorities, and thinking style. The methods we've discussed (listening for Word Clues, meta-programs, and overall language use) are relatively weak on their own, but become incredibly powerful when combined. You can use these methods strategically, focusing and targeting your questions to confirm or disprove certain working hypotheses.

Have you ever heard people say that they've spoken to someone for hours, or even known them for years, and yet they actually know nothing about them? That's because their conversation lacked strategy and focus. With a little practice and awareness, though, you can be the opposite—you will be able to talk to people for an astonishingly short amount of time and yet see more clearly into the depths of who they are as a person.

Here are a few last hints and tips for asking questions that will help you fine-tune your people-reading skills:

- As a rule, begin with open-ended questions and lead to more closed ones once the flow of conversation is established. This neatly maps on to asking more chunking up questions first, and then after you've gained an overview (and the person is more comfortable with you), you can drill a little deeper with a closed question that probes for a specific, detailed answer.

- Be careful not to ask too many questions (of any kind). It will feel like an interview or interrogation, and the person will definitely register that the exchange of information is imbalanced.
- Try posing some questions as statements—for example, "You're one of those super smart people, so I bet you learned all sorts of amazing things while living there." Such statements act as questions since they spur conversation and inspire the other person to tell you what you want to know. Extra points if you can be a little unexpected or controversial—the way people jump in to respond tells you a lot about where they are psychologically: "Smart!? Well, I certainly didn't feel that way at the time. Quite the opposite, actually..."

Finally, one tip is to work on the delivery of questions. When you ask, use a friendly, relaxed tone of voice, without eye contact, and then once you've asked the question, pause and make eye contact—this body language acts like a nonverbal invitation for them to speak, and communicates your respectful interest in their answer, without being pushy. Likewise, pay attention to their eye contact. Avoiding your gaze or looking away may suggest their wanting to avoid that question!

Summary:

- A great way to get information about a person is to ask targeted questions. The best questions are those that appear on the surface to be asking about something unrelated.
- We can use the Kipling method (5W1H—who, what, where, when, why, and how) to help us structure our efforts to gather information that will help us understand a person better.
- An assumptive question is one that forces certain assumptions and thus implies something about the form the answer could take. The way someone responds to these implications can speak volumes, so notice what they focus on and what they dismiss. The questions that people ask *you* can also reveal their own assumptions, biases, and preconceptions.
- "Chunking" is the way information is grouped into bigger or smaller pieces. The way people use chunking in their own speech or respond to your

chunking can tell you interesting things about them.
- "Chunking up" is moving from specific and detailed information to more general or abstract information and can signal detachment or critical thinking, while "chunking down" inquires about details and specifics and can signal interest or more concrete thinking. Notice the person's chunking style and how they respond to yours.
- Keep questions open-ended and varied and don't ask too many. Try to pose some questions as statements and note the response. Ask with a friendly tone and maintain eye contact, leaving enough space for an answer.

www.ingramcontent.com/pod-product-compliance
Lightning Source LLC
Chambersburg PA
CBHW020528080526
44583CB00013B/782